# The Evangelistic Church

## by John F. Havlik

CONVENTION PRESS
A CHURCH SERVICES AND MATERIALS DIVISION PRODUCT

# A personal message
## from the author

The Church Administration Department of The Sunday School Board and the Department of Evangelism Development in the Evangelism Section of the Home Mission Board have worked together on an emphasis on growth evangelism for the 1976-77 church year. Growth evangelism involves the concept of equipping Christians to mature in their faith and effectively share their faith. As a result, the Lord has a suitable climate in which to add to his church those that are being saved. The state secretaries of evangelism approved the emphasis. They determined that major attention would be placed on bringing back into fellowship and service the thousands of resident inactive members of our churches. Church administration leaders asked to join us in this emphasis. We decided to stress the place of the deacon in evangelism. Pastors and deacons will study this book together. Then, deacons will teach the book in a spiritual life conference sometime in the months of January to March 1977.

This book is really not a book on methods. It is a theology-vision of an evangelistic church. All the books on church growth and evangelism today point to Southern Baptists as a large denomination that has retained its evangelistic zeal and effectiveness. While this gives all of us joy and pride in what the Lord has done through us, we still have to see the scene as it really is. Some of our churches have settled into a dull routine that is unexciting and unappealing. The joy and celebration over evangelistic victories have been lost in the flat sameness of service after service. Some of our churches (especially in the cities) have not learned how to communicate with a secular society. Some of our churches exist as a well-insulated little pocket of spirituality in the midst of a sea of indifference. The world does not hate us. They do not love us. They do not know we are here. The church has inadequate effect on political, social, economic, or even moral issues in the cities. There is a great need for renewal for every believer and revival for the people of God.

There are many "parable" churches in the Southern Baptist Convention. They are dynamic, growing churches. They are both large and small, city and rural, rich and poor. Most of the insights

The first gospel sermon that John Havlik remembers hearing was preached by Gypsy Smith in Tulsa, Oklahoma. He was converted in a tent revival where B. B. McKinney was leading the music. Havlik is the director of the department of Evangelism Development in the Evangelism Section of the Home Mission Board.

in this book have come from watching these churches grow while others around them were struggling to exist. The pastors of these churches are just as different as the churches. They are not all unusually gifted men. I think I have detected some commonalities about these pastors and churches. They are:

1) Pastors who have a vision of growing an evangelistic church and are able to effectively communicate the vision.
2) Pastors who genuinely like people.
3) People who have genuine concern about the relationship that other people have to God.
4) People who as a matter of life-style witness-visit naturally and with a feeling of security.
5) Churches that are pluralistic by choice. They are open to all kinds of persons with varying life-styles. There are no racial, cultural, or language barriers.
6) Pastors and staffs that are able to administrate a process of empowering, equipping, and enabling believers for loving, Christlike evangelistic ministry.

This book is about these six things. Most of the content comes from my own biblical studies, my experiences as a guest in many of the growing evangelistic churches in our Convention, and my personal observations of these pastors and churches. I am indebted to Lyle Schaller for his lectures to the staff of the Home Mission Board. The following books have been helpful and worth reading in the area of church growth and innovative evangelistic ministries. The literature on these topics is inexhaustive. Some have been more helpful than others. The two books by Donald A. MacGavran, *How Churches Grow* and *Understanding Church Growth* are very useful. Lewis A. Drummond, professor of evangelism at Southern Seminary, authored an excellent book, *Leading Your Church in Evangelism.* Ralph W. Neighbour and Cal Thomas collaborated on a good book on new and innovative ministries called *Target Group Evangelism.* Donald J. McNair wrote *The Growing Local Church.* Paul Benjamin, professor at Lincoln Christian College, has two small but useful books, *The Growing Congregation* and *How in the World?* A very useful and scholarly book that takes a hard look at church structures and organizations is Lawrence O. Richards' *A Theology of Christian Education*. Pastors, deacons, and study groups interested in further studies might find these books interesting.

I am especially indebted to the staff and people of the First Baptist Church, Chamblee, Georgia. I supplied their pulpit several Sundays while they were seeking a pastor. I preached a great deal about the vision, discipleship, and the evangelistic church and used them as a forum for many of the ideas in this book. They were good listeners and responded with enthusiasm to some of the things I had to say and have tried to say again in this book.

O God, give us the vision, Amen.

John F. Havlik, *Director*
*Department of Evangelism Development*
*Home Mission Board*
*Atlanta, Georgia*

# Contents

# CHAPTER 1

I. Evangelism Is a Message and a Mission
  1. Evangelism Cannot Be Separated from Theology
  2. Evangelism Cannot Be Separated from the Concerns of This Life
  3. Evangelism Must Be Understood by the Layperson
II. Evangelism Is God's Eternal Purpose
  1. Evangelism Is God's Saving Purpose in the Old Testament
  2. Evangelism Is What God Has Done in Jesus Christ
III. Evangelism Is Good News
  1. Evangelism Is the Good News About God's Initiative
  2. Evangelism Is the Good News About God's Kingdom
IV. Evangelism Is a Task
V. Evangelism Is Evangelizing and Equipping
  1. Evangelism Is Evangelizing and Equipping Christians to Evangelize
  2. The Church in Acts Is a Model Evangelistic Church
VI. Evangelism Is the Word and the Deed
  1. Products Must Be Consistent with Proclamation
  2. A Hurtful Heresy to Evangelism
  3. Actualizing the Word into Deeds

# 1
# What Is Evangelism?

Evangelism with a capital "E" is on the world's agenda today.. Everyone is trying to win everyone else to something or other. We are literally drenched in one kind of propaganda or another. The media, openly or subconsciously, attempt to make converts to products, ideas, and ideals. Groups of persons, such as minorities, manufacturers, laborers, political parties, and persons with differing life-styles are literally bombarding us with both the hard and soft sell. No generation of this planet's population has believed so gullibly and dangerously as ours. The world's people are now believing in gods that are not gods. Music, the fine arts, the dramatic arts, and literature are all used as mediums to soften up the populace for the abandonment of moral and ethical values which humanity has taken centuries to develop. Communism is a winner in many parts of our world. Islam is a winner among some young black Americans. Soka Gakkai is a winner in Japan. Christians engaged in evangelism need to understand that we face stiff competition for the minds and hearts of humanity.

## I. Evangelism Is a Message and a Mission

Though evangelism may not yet be a clear call to man the lifeboats in the average church, it is now on the agenda of the church. Since the early seventies, evangelism has been in the air. There is a need for getting it "on the ground" as well. There is a need for a down-to-earth theology of evangelism. The reawakening of the laity in the seventies demands a theology of evangelism without all the technicalities of the theologians. There is also a need for evangelism to become involved with the concerns of humanity in this life. Too much of what we say about evangelism and even the evangelistic message is often obscured in theological jargon of the eighteenth century and an otherworldly preoccupation that alienates it from the modern mind-set and life-style. People are saying, "Keep it simple." They are also asking, "What will it do for me today?" The message of the New Testament is a propaganda message. It was meant to be understood and believed by the common man.

### 1. Evangelism Cannot Be Separated from Theology

One of the difficulties here is that generally teachers of theology and pastors are skeptical of evangelists and evangelists are skeptical of teachers of theology and pastors. Evangelists feel that teachers of theology and pastors often obscure the simplicity of the gospel with a lot of technical and theological language. Teachers of theology and pastors often feel that evangelists oversimplify the gospel and offer a "cheap grace." In spite of this, we cannot separate evangelism and theology because they are never separated in the Scriptures. Message and mission are so interwoven in the Scriptures that they cannot be separated. An example is the message and mission of Christ. Who he was, what he came to do, and what he said are so intermixed that we cannot talk about one without talking about the other.

A further reason why theology and evangelism cannot be separated is that they were not separated by those leaders who have most influenced the church throughout its history. Paul, Augustine, Luther, and Wesley were the theologians who drastically changed the theology and direction of the church. They were also evangelists. When Luther was asked, "What should we preach?" he answered directly, firmly, and succinctly, "The gospel." His definition of evangelism was to bring Christ to men and men to Christ.

A separation of evangelism and theology would kill them both. There is nothing as inane and meaningless as a theology without evangelism. To believe something as great as God's love in Jesus Christ and not want to share it with others with excitement is unbelievable. On the other hand, there is nothing more shallow or empty than a purely emotional appeal to a cheap kind of grace that really doesn't take Christ and his cross seriously. Evangelism needs theology, and theology needs evangelism.

### 2. Evangelism Cannot Be Separated from the Concerns of This Life

Our example is none other than our Lord himself. He did not separate his concern for our future life and our life here and now. Jesus never made salvation a pie-in-the-sky-by-and-by proposition. He was interested in both breaking the shackles of a person's present slavery and delivering him from eternal hell. Jesus announced that he did not come into the world to be served, but to serve and to give his life as a purchase price (see Matt. 20:28). In this announcement, Jesus linked together in the closest of relationships his ministry to man's need and his sacrificial death. He came to live so that we can die, having peace with God. He came to die so that we can live in fellowship with God and with one another.

Jesus Christ is concerned about human kinds of things. He was concerned because a woman had a bleeding tumor (Matt. 9:20). He was concerned because people were hungry and tired (Matt. 12:1-3). He was concerned because a father grieved for a dead daughter (Matt. 9:18). He didn't say to these hurting people, "I can't be bothered with your earthly problems; I am only interested in your 'soul.'" He helped them where they hurt. Paul was also a good example of this. It has been said that Paul began every epistle in the heavenlies and ended them in the kitchen. It is very true that Paul was not preoccupied with the life beyond. What we have tried to establish is that evangelism cannot be separated from theology, and it cannot be separated from man's life in this world.

### 3. Evangelism Must Be Understood by Laypersons

An ancillary but important thought is that evangelism must keep its theology biblical, simple, and readily understood by the layperson.

## II. Evangelism Is God's Eternal Purpose

God's purpose and power to redeem is not the exclusive possession of Christians.

### 1. Evangelism Is God's Saving Purpose in the Old Testament

Israel, as the people of God, had been created in a great historic act of God's saving grace. By an act of God, they were redeemed from Egyptian bondage. They had been set free. Later, God saved this same "peculiar" people from exile in Babylon. His saving power and purpose is at the very heart of evangelism. The five centuries from the fall of Jerusalem to the birth of Jesus were used of God to bring the world of humanity to a time of "fullness." The fine arts had reached their fullness in Greece. Government and law had reached their fullness in Rome. Religion had reached its fullness in Judaism. In contrast to these human achievements one third of the world were slaves. Sensuality had ripened into a nightmare of obsession with sex and sexual perversion in Rome. People were searching for answers by turning to mystical religions and sects. "But when the fulness of time came, God sent forth His Son, born of a woman, born under the Law, in order that He might redeem those who were under the Law, that we might receive the adoption as sons" (Gal. 4:4-5, NASB).[1]

### 2. Evangelism Is What God Has Done in Jesus Christ

Evangelism is the incredible good news of what God has done by his mightiest of all acts in Jesus Christ. "God, after he spoke long ago to the fathers in the prophets in many portions and in many ways, in these last days has spoken to us in His Son, . . . through whom also He made the world" (Heb. 1:1-2, NASB). Evangelism is that message verbalized by human lips and "fleshed out" in human lives. The "ism" ending on the word itself indicates action and life. It is not a static message. It is not a message "saved up." It is the message preached, whispered, shouted, spoken, sung, printed, displayed, and parabled. It is "news that is too good to keep." Every member of the church in Jerusalem considered the "preaching of the good news" as his responsibility. Persecution forced believers to flee for their lives. The apostles remained in Jerusalem (Acts 8:1). Then Luke tells us that "those who had been scattered went about preaching the word" (Acts 8:4, NASB). Phillip, the deacon, was among those who had been scattered by persecution. Evangelism is the good news that all believers are responsible for announcing. We have a right to ask, "What is this good news about?"

Everyone is bombarding everyone else with both the hard and soft sell. Even music, the fine arts, the dramatic arts, and literature are used as mediums to soften up the populace for the abandonment of moral and ethical values which humanity has taken centuries to develop.

## III. Evangelism Is Good News

There are recurring phrases in the New Testament in which the good news is identified and defined. The salvation acts of God had taken place in the past. In Christ we have the finale, the last act in the drama of redemption (Heb. 1:1-2). The gospel is the good news about salvation in Christ. It is the gospel of God (Mark 1:15; Rom. 15:16; 2 Cor. 11:7; 1 Thess. 2:2,8-9; 1 Pet. 4:17).

### 1. Evangelism Is the Good News About God's Initiative

The good news has it origin in God's everlasting mercy. The initiative is his. He loved us before we loved him. The good news of salvation brings glory to God, so it is the "glorious gospel of the blessed God" (1 Tim. 1:11). The salvation of God was preached by Jesus of Nazareth. It was about Jesus of Nazareth. God's salvation was accomplished by Jesus of Nazareth. It is the "gospel of Christ" (Rom. 15:19; 1 Cor. 9:12; 2 Cor. 2:12; 2 Cor. 9:13; 2 Cor. 10:14; Phil. 1:27). It is the good news by Christ, about Christ, and in Christ. It is the "gospel of our Lord Jesus Christ" (2 Thess. 1:8). It is the gospel of the Son of God (Rom. 1:9). It is the "gospel of the glory of Christ" (2 Cor. 4:4, RSV).

### 2. Evangelism Is the Good News About God's Kingdom

The gospel is good news about the kingdom—God's reign over persons and created things, God's new social order (Matt. 4:23; Matt. 9:35; Matt. 24:14). It is good news that persons do not have to be beasts, constantly tearing at one another. The "new morality" of the kingdom is set out in the Sermon on the Mount. The gospel is good news for those who need it, want it, and take it by faith. It is the good news of "your salvation" (Eph. 1:13). Because there are gracious and good consequences in receiving and believing the gospel, it is the "gospel of peace" and the gospel of hope (Eph. 6:15; Col. 1:23). The gospel when received is utterly undeserved. It is a gospel for sinners. It is the gospel of the "grace of God" (Acts 20:24). It is the incredible news that God is making all things new. The experience of receiving the gospel is called a new birth (John 3:3). Those who experience God's salvation in Jesus Christ are called new creatures (2 Cor. 5:17). Even the world of nature is included in God's great plan of making all things new so that there will be a "new heaven and a new earth" (Rev. 21:1).

## IV. Evangelism Is a Task

Before Christ's ascension, he gave the church a task. Go into the whole world and *make* disciples, *mark* disciples (with the ordinance of baptism) and *mature* disciples (teaching them to put into practice everything that he said) (see Matt. 28:19-20).

Paul wrote to the young pastor, Timothy, and said, "Do the work of an evangelist" (2 Tim. 4:5). Paul said that the risen Christ gave gifts to persons and then gave those persons to the church "for the equipping of the saints for the work of service" (Eph. 4:12, NASB). This points up the fact that growing a church in Christian maturity and in numbers is work.

The pastor-teacher has a work of equipping the saints. The people have a work of serving. All of this relates to evangelism as a task. In launching lay evangelism schools in our churches, two things were discovered. First, the average layperson has a greater desire to be used in evangelism than church leaders realize. Church leaders need to renew their faith in laypersons. The second thing we discovered was that laypersons require a great deal more help and equipping than most church leaders believe. Some pastors apparently assume that because a man has expertise in a secular task, he can automatically do the work of evangelism if properly motivated. This is far from true.

Joe came to a lay evangelism school that I was teaching in his church. He is assistant to the president of a large corporation. He had successfully organized and conducted a gubernatorial campaign in a large state. He is a "football type," large, well-built, and good-looking. He is a real extrovert. Joe was present every evening. He was an enthusiastic participant in the creative activities, an eager listener to all the lectures, and an apt pupil for the practical activities. After the school on Wednesday evening, I tried to prepare everyone for the lab-witness on Thursday evening. Joe came to me and said, "I am literally scared to death. I wonder if I could go with you and watch you witness to someone, and then I'll be able to do it." I agreed, even though I usually make it a practice to be the "silent partner." Our prospect was John Singleton, who had been visited often by members of the church. His wife and his two sons were members of the church. Before we left the church to make our call, I talked to someone who knew John Singleton. They told me that he was very proud of his two teenage sons.

Since Joe had met John, I asked him to introduce me as "John Havlik," not as a preacher or a denominational person.

Singleton was at home alone, watching television. The first thing I noticed after our introduction was the pictures of the two boys on top of the television set. I sat on a chair near Singleton, and Joe sat on a sofa across the room. Looking at the pictures, I asked, "John, are those your boys? They certainly are fine looking."

He answered, "Yes, those are my boys, and I am very proud of them. They are good boys."

I said, "Mr. Singleton, Joe and I have been attending a lay evangelism school. We have discovered a little booklet that says what we would like to say to you. I know many people have talked to you about becoming a Christian, including several preachers. I would like to just read through this little booklet. It is called, 'How to Have a Full and Meaningful Life.' " [2] Pushing my chair over beside his, I said, "Do you mind if Joe turns off the TV so we can hear what this little booklet is saying to us?" "No," he said, "turn it off. Most of the time I wonder why I listen to it." I read through the booklet.

When I came to the prayer of commitment, I asked John Singleton if this was the kind of prayer he had really wanted to pray. He said he would pray the prayer and make the commitment. I then asked him to read through the remainder of the booklet, including some Scripture passages on assurance and church membership. He agreed to come the following Sunday to unite with the church. Then I said, "Mr. Singleton, I am going to give you this booklet. All I did was read it to you, and you have committed your life to Jesus Christ. Do you think you could read it to one of your friends?" He replied that he thought he could and mentioned the name of a friend he worked with.

After we got outside the home, Joe said to me, "You know, I can do that." He then thought for a moment and said, "Anyone who is a Christian can do that."

In addition to his outgoing personality and his ability to meet and talk to people, Joe needed much more help than a rousing sermon on witnessing. Indeed, the pastor should continue preaching sermons on witnessing, but the average person needs special help.

Evangelism is more than a message; it is a task. It is a task for disciples, and disciples are made, not born. The business of the church is making disciples. Salvation is a work of the Holy

Spirit, and the Spirit is making persons new. The new person born of the Spirit is to be discipled. Although he is a personal follower of Jesus Christ, he may not become a real disciple unless he is taught. Jesus called persons to himself. He then took two years to constantly teach them to be disciples. What Joe discovered in the lay evangelism school was empowering, equipping, encouraging. He had an opportunity to "try out his new wings" in company with another disciple. What Joe really needed was some skills in presenting the gospel and some equipping (discipling), including motivation to use his acquired skills.

## V. Evangelism Is Evangelizing and Equipping

The task of the evangelistic church actually involves two things—evangelizing every person in the community and equipping (discipling) every person who is converted to Jesus Christ.

### 1. *Evangelizing and Equipping Christians to Evangelize*

It is impossible to have an evangelistic church without both evangelizing and equipping. Many churches believe that all they need is an evangelistic pastor. He may only serve to make the church uncomfortable if they are not equipped to evangelize. God's salvation is a response to man's need. The gospel is the good news that God has met that need in Jesus Christ. To announce that gospel to persons and give them opportunity to respond is evangelizing. Christians are to follow Jesus Christ. This means that his mission is our mission.

Christians living Christ's life, accomplishing his mission, and accepting his ministry are disciples. This is apparent in the commission in Matthew's and Mark's Gospels. In Mark the accent of the commission is on evangelizing. "And He said to them, 'Go into all the world and preach the gospel to all creation'" (Mark 16:15, NASB). In Matthew the accent is on discipling to evangelize. "Go therefore and make disciples of all the nations [peoples], baptizing them . . . teaching them to observe [to put into practice] all that I commanded you" (Matt. 28:19-20, NASB). Discipling involves leading people *to put into practice* all that Christ commanded us to do. It is both being and doing. We do certain things because of what we are. The Christian is a disciple, and he disciples. He is a witness, and he witnesses. He is good, and he does good things.

The emphasis in discipling is on "being." The emphasis in evangelizing is on "doing."

Our real problem in developing evangelistic churches is that we emphasize one or the other. To emphasize only one is to neglect the other. A church may emphasize the preaching of the message. The preaching is done by the evangelistic pastor and visiting evangelists. The testimonies of successful persons in the athletic and entertainment fields are often used. This may be an effective approach. However, this approach to evangelism should not be used as a gimmick just to attract the curious. When this is the case, many "decisions" may be recorded that have little or no continuing relationship with the church. No disciples are being made. What this church has done is to substitute the one-to-one method of the New Testament for an inadequate substitute in getting hearers for public proclamation. This church goes from one spiritual high to another without really adding those who are saved (disciples) to the church.

Another church may emphasize "being good" and place a strong emphasis on renewal, the deeper life, and living Spirit-filled lives. I was asked to lead revival services in such a church. The members were people of prayer. They studied their Bibles faithfully. They carefully jotted down notes in the margins of their Bibles when I preached. They practiced a degree of separation from the world that was admirable. *But the church had not baptized a single convert in three years.* They were good, but good for what?

Another church may emphasize "doing good." They are social activists in on every kind of good work that exists in the community. They insist that they do not need to verbalize the gospel because everyone will "see Jesus" in them. Sometimes they really do not do a lot of good; they just talk about it. The pulpit sounds out on all the social issues, but they are actually not involved. In either case their specialty is doing good or talking about doing good. They make very few converts.

*Churches need to "get it all together."* Evangelism is "being good." It is "doing good." It is confronting men with the claims of Christ. It is all of these things. Evangelism is not riding hobby horses named "gifts," "discipling," "Spirit filled" or "just preach the gospel." Evangelism is making, baptizing, and teaching disciples. Evangelism includes all the "hobby horses" in their proper perspective and balance. The name of that game is *growing an evangelistic church.*

### 2. The Church in Acts Is a Model Evangelistic Church

Churches are not evangelistic accidentally but deliberately. The church in Acts is a case in point. In chapter 1 the waiting church received the evangelistic commission to cross all barriers to evangelize (Acts 1:8). They were to go to the big city (Jerusalem). They were to go to other religions (Judea). They were to go to other races (the Samaritans). They were to go to the whole world.

In chapter 2 they were empowered and equipped. Peter's sermon and the witnessing of the disciples among the crowds gathered for Pentecost resulted in thousands of new disciples who were added to the church.

In chapters 3 to 5, evangelism continued to dominate their activities so that "all the more believers in the Lord, multitudes of men and women, were constantly added to their number" (Acts 5:14, NASB).

In chapter 6, seven men were chosen to take care of some needed ministries within the church so that others could give themselves to witnessing and preaching. "And the word of God kept on spreading; and the number of the disciples continued to increase greatly in Jerusalem, and a great many of the priests were becoming obedient to the faith" (Acts 6:7, NASB).

Chapter 9 tells of the conversion of Saul of Tarsus and the spread of the church from Jerusalem. "So the church throughout all Judea and Galilee and Samaria enjoyed peace, being built up; and, going on in the fear of the Lord and in the comfort of the Holy Spirit, *it continued to increase*" (Acts 9:21, NASB).

In chapters 9 through 11, a Gentile was converted, and Peter was relieved of some of his feelings of superiority over other races. The disciples were amazed to see evangelism even more fruitful among the Gentiles than it had been among the Jews.

In chapter 13, from Antioch, the center of evangelistic activity, Paul was sent on his first mission. "And as many as had been appointed to eternal life believed. And the word of the Lord was being spread through the whole region" (Acts 13:48-49).

The story goes on through the book of Acts. This church deliberately put priority on evangelism. Unless church leaders and churches are willing to be committed to this kind of biblical priority, the church will not be evangelistic.

## VI. Evangelism Is the Word and the Deed

In Jesus Christ the word became the deed in flesh and blood (John 1:14). It is important to the point of desperation that the word and the deed not be divided. It is especially important today.

### 1. Products Must Be Consistent with Proclamation

In the late sixties and early seventies there was incredible pressure placed upon government and industry to produce actions and products consistent with the claims of advertising. Campaign promises are remembered today. If advertising promises a detergent that will make our clothes twice as bright, as consumers we want a product that will do it. For a long time the church has made claims as to what Jesus Christ can do. The thinking unbeliever hears us promise that Jesus Christ will make a person love his neighbor as himself. They see and read about Protestants and Catholics killing each other in Ireland and Moslem and Christian warring in the Middle East. The thinking unbeliever hears radio preachers talk about God's love out of one side of their mouths and rant against fellow Christians out of the other. They hear Jesus say, "Feed the poor," but the poor go unfed. They visit churches with $50,000 crystal chandeliers in cities where thousands are hungry. They hear Jesus say, "Bless them that curse you," and then see Christians in a traffic jam with veins standing out of their foreheads shouting, "Same to you, brother!" They hear us talk about sacrificial giving for home and foreign missions, and they know that what we give per capita is equal to about three hamburgers or three packages of cigarettes.

The good news that the angels sang over the field of the shepherds on that night of nights was the good news that a concerned God became flesh and blood. The Word was Christ, who went about doing good. Preaching and performance cannot mock each other. We have a tendency to preach about the incarnation as if it were a magnificent obsession and live as if it were an unrealistic dream. In the judgment scene in Matthew 25:31-46, Jesus pictured two kinds of persons: those who inherited the prepared kingdom and had demonstrated their faith through ministry; and those who were cut off from God eternally and had rejected God and lived

Evangelism is the Word and the deed. The Word becomes the deed, and that is good news. It is good news when a concerned Christian becomes a big brother to some fatherless child in the ghetto.

for themselves with no thought of ministry. It is utterly impossible to separate evangelism from ethics. Consider how much of the New Testament speaks to Christian behavior. Paul in his epistles holds our relationship to others in every order of society under the searchlight of truth. This includes our relationships in the home, the church, the city, the state, the nation, and the world. According to Paul's teachings, a person's emotions, behavior, attitudes, and actions are all to be brought under the dominion of Christ.

### 2. A Hurtful Heresy to Evangelism

The sneaky, subtle, and insidious heresy that hurts our evangelism more than any one thing is the idea that the life of holiness is only for those who are ordained or in some special way set apart for Christian service. This is the heresy that constantly comes to the surface in our church life in spite of our continued avowal of the doctrine of the priesthood of all believers. We see our sins, and we know that they are wrong; but we take a certain pride in saying, "Well, thank God, at least I am not a Pharisee." We feel good about the fact that we go to church; we help pay the bills to keep "the kingdom" going. We even say a prayer now and then. Even the preachers sometimes help us stay in our condition of half-hearted Christian service by saying, "Well, he's just a layman." The call to discipleship, to holiness, to ministry, and to brotherhood is for all of us. We have overworked the biblical calling for the ordained and ignored it for the unordained. Jesus calls us all to a life of commitment, compassion, and conviction. Christians, whose daily lives deny the truth of Christ, do more harm to evangelism than the secular forces outside the church. When the word becomes the deed, the Person becomes the pattern. Jesus Christ is the Person. The pattern is his life in us. Christian ethics as a system of injunctions cannot save us. Jesus Christ can. This is the good news. When we speak the good news and our lives fail to reflect the pattern, it is bad news. All of us are called to the same Christlife.

### 3. Actualizing the Word into Deeds

When Christ is truly in our lives, we are Christlike. When we really love, we do loving things. When we have known the Everlasting Mercy, we do merciful things. When his compassion fills our hearts, we do compassionate things. The word becomes the deed, and that actualizes the good news into deeds. That is evangelism. The star of Bethlehem ran an evangelistic errand on that night of nights. The shepherds heard an evangelistic anthem sung by an angelic choir. Wise men came from the east at the beckoning of the evangelistic star. It was good news. It is good news when a Christian loves an alcoholic up out of his drunken hell. It is good news when some loving Christian teaches the unloved and unloving how to love and be loved. It is good news when a concerned Christian teaches an international person the English language. It is good news when some solid, concerned Christian becomes a "big brother" to some fatherless child in the ghetto. It is good news when Christians begin to apply what they believe to the hurts of humanity. When we practice this kind of Christianity, we are practicing the teachings of Christ. Let the word become the deed.

Our most difficult task in evangelizing the world is to convince the world that Jesus Christ can make life better. This is difficult because of our Christian inconsistencies being viewed by a doubting world. The greatest evidence that Jesus Christ can make persons new is the life of the believer lived openly before others. Successful evangelism waits upon holy, Christlike living. One of the greatest devotional, life-changing disciplines is to study the life of Jesus Christ. I do not mean a harmony of the Gospels or studying the events of the Judean, Perean, and Galilean ministries. Take the Gospels, particularly Luke, and just read what Jesus said and did—how he loved people, helped people, exposed hypocrisy, stood for justice, showed compassion to the poor, ministered to the sick, and loved children. Study what he said and did, and then study it again and again until it becomes a part of life's actions. Our words should become living commentaries on the life of Christ. He said God loved the world so much that God gave his Son. Then he wrote that love in his own blood on a hill outside Jerusalem for all the world to see. *That is evangelism.*

A book that has meant very much to me is *Creative Brooding* by Robert Raines. Pray one of Raines' prayers with me:

*O God, make me love justice,*
*    and seek equal job opportunity where I work,*
*    open housing in my apartment building or suburb,*
*    open membership in my club,*
*        better schools for all children in my city.*

O God, make me hate wrong,
   and speak out against it boldly,
   at parties,
   among my relatives,
   in my church board meetings,
   at work.
O God, keep me from being contentious,
   but make me care enough to contend
      for justice,
      against wrong
         with humility.[3]

## Review

Evangelism is on the agenda of the church. There is widespread interest in evangelism. There is a need for coming to a theology of evangelism that communicates with the layperson in the church and with secular persons. Evangelism and theology are not separated in the Scriptures. The persons who most influenced Christian history were the theologians who were evangelists. Evangelism cannot be separated from the concerns of this life. Christ is interested in our whole life.

Evangelism is the eternal purpose of God. God's desire and will to save humanity has its roots in the Old Testament. Evangelism reveals God's eternal saving purpose in Jesus Christ. Evangelism is the message of what God has done in Jesus Christ, verbalized and "fleshed out" in human life. Evangelism is a message—"the good news." It is the good news about God. It is the good news that brings glory to God. It is the good news about Jesus Christ. It is the good news about our salvation. Evangelism is a task as well as a message. The task of evangelism involves evangelizing those who are out of Christ and equipping believers for witness-ministry. The church in the book of Acts is an example of a church evangelizing the non-Christian and equipping the believers.

## Questions for Discussion

1. The author discusses the stiff competition the church faces in the world. What competitive forces exist in your community that ask for the priority loyalties of persons?
2. The author discusses the need to make the church a "lay seminary" to equip the laypersons for ministry. Is this too idealistic?

Is it possible? If it is, how might it be done?
3. The gospel is good news. How can we *be* the good news as well as *verbalize* the good news?
4. Churches are not evangelistic accidentally but purposively. What steps has your church taken to be purposively evangelistic?
5. Evangelism is a priority task of the church. What priority has your church given evangelism? Does your budget reflect this? Does your bulletin reflect this? Does your witness-visitation program reflect this? Does your baptismal record reflect this?

---

[1] From the *New American Standard Bible.* © The Lockman Foundation, La Habra, California, 1971. Published by Creation House, Inc., Carol Stream, Illinois. All succeeding quotations from this version are indicated by the abbreviation NASB in parentheses.

[2] This and other WIN (Witness Involvement Now) materials are available from Materials Services Department, The Sunday School Board, Nashville, Tennessee 37234.

[3] Reprinted with permission of Macmillan Publishing Co., Inc. from *Creative Brooding.* Copyright © Robert A. Raines, 1966.

# CHAPTER 2

# 2
# The Evangelistic Church

The church is the medium of communicating the gospel message.

## I. What the Evangelistic Church Communicates

We learned from a review of the book of Acts that the church, not "spiritual stars," bears the message of salvation. It is true that there are great men such as Paul, but he built no reputation for himself. Indeed, he counted reputation as nothing.

### 1. *The Church Is the Medium for Communicating the Message*
The early church in Acts communicated the message and equipped the people of God. The evangelizing of our world will either be done by the church or will not be done at all. The church is the body of Jesus Christ (1 Cor. 6:15; 1 Cor. 12:12; Eph. 1:22; Eph. 4:12; Col. 1:18-24; Rom. 12:5). These passages are critical for an understanding of the mission of the church.

### 2. *The Church Is on Christ's Mission*
Why was God incarnate in Jesus Christ? Why did God want a body to walk around in this world? Christ himself answers this question. In several terse announcements, he stated the purpose of his coming into the world. He came into the world to find and save persons who are lost (Luke 19:10). He came into the world to call sinners to repentance (Matt. 9:13). He came into the world to establish a new standard of righteousness (Matt. 5:17). He came

into the world to minister (serve) and to die (Matt. 20:28). The mission of the church then is to announce that Jesus Christ is Lord. The response to that announcement is to be one of life and death. It is life for those who submit to his lordship. It is death for those who refuse to believe and submit to his lordship. Those who hear and believe are to follow Christ, love him, and obey him above all other leaders, loves, and loyalties, even above parents or marriage partners. Believers are to be baptized and taught to put into practice the new standard of righteousness. They are to become ministers even to the death of self. The evangelized become evangelists.

### 3. The Church Communicates the Gospel by What It Is and What It Does

All too often our theology and our actions deny rather than confirm one another. An example is our evangelistic methods. We say that every member is a minister. We preach the priesthood of the believer. We teach that every Christian is an evangelist. Then we ask the believers to become spectators at an evangelistic production and finally to pay for the "show." Consequently people are not reached through the one-to-one ministry. When the evangelistic effort is over, we may have nothing more than a display of beauty contest winners or prominent athletes that place the layperson in an inactive spectator role. We may have succeeded in getting a crowd, but at what price?

Another example is a church getting into a hassle. They may gossip and even lie about one another while the preacher is preaching his heart out about "God is love." These inconsistencies are harmful to a world that watches and wonders.

Jesus communicated his mission by what he was and what he did. Are we communicating that same mission with clarity and conviction? Are we communicating the truth that Jesus Christ is Lord? Are we clearly communicating that we care about people?

I recently preached at a downtown church just a half block from the favorite gathering and drinking place for winos. When I got out of my car, I saw a young man with his open Bible talking earnestly to some of the winos. I asked him if he belonged to the church where I was preaching. "No," he replied. "I belong to a church in the suburbs. But I come down here every Sunday morning because it's a good place to witness." I went inside the church. By the time the service was over I heard four people complaining how the church was dying. They said it was being killed "by those awful people sitting out there on the edge of the parking lot." What was this church communicating? What was the young man communicating? Do we see people as opportunities and persons for whom Christ died? For the young man, the winos were an opportunity; for that church, they were an embarrassment.

What the church is and what the church does can communicate the mission of Christ and our mission, or it can communicate something very different and even in opposition to that mission. Christ came to find and save persons who are lost. Is our church open to people? Does it reflect a seeking love that goes out to people by what it is and what it does? Jesus came into the world to talk with, eat with, and go home with sinners. Does our church attract "nice people like us," or does it really reflect what it claims to be—a fellowship of sinners? Christ came into the world to make his claim as Lord. Does our church reflect that Jesus Christ is Lord, or do we in subtle ways communicate that we have to have it our way? He came into the world to establish a new standard of righteousness taught in the Sermon on the Mount. How well does our church reflect the Beatitudes of our Lord? Are we happy in being the children of God, pure of heart, merciful, and meek? Jesus came into the world to minister and to die. How well does our church communicate the death of self and a commitment to serve humanity? How much are we involved with those movements and programs designed to give men a better life? All of these questions are pertinent for church leaders as they pray and plan for an evangelistic church. The church as the body of Jesus Christ is in the world to complete his mission. He says, "As the Father has sent Me, I also send you" (John 20:21, NASB).

## II. What the Evangelistic Church Is

The early church was constantly giving themselves to one another in the teaching of the apostles, in sharing their common life, in the symbolism of the Lord's table, and in prayer. Everyone stood in awe at the wonderful things that were happening. All those who had believed came together and shared everything they had with one another, even their property and possessions (see Acts 2:42-45). Does this sound like our church? Remember that this

The evangelistic church communicates its concerns by its actions. Instead of just trying to attract "nice people like us," churches are challenged to reach out to the underprivileged.

is the evangelistic church whose history we reviewed in chapter 1. The very nature of evangelism is sharing the gospel with others. The evangelistic church is a sharing fellowship. Christians and churches who have never learned to share with one another can hardly be expected to be adept and comfortable in sharing with persons outside the fellowship. Sharing, like judgment and salvation, must begin at the household of faith. The church can carry on a charade of sharing, "shouting the gospel" to an uncaring world, while inside the church people either do not know each other and they are glad they don't, or they do know each other and they are sorry they do. A church like this usually has a compulsion to preach in a louder voice, and, as in the old song "Paper Moon," it is "a melody played in a penny arcade, a Barnum and Bailey world as phony as it can be." If our only bond is orthodox doctrine, then we are a partisan religious sect. If our only bond is our interest in our suburban middle-class community, then we are a country club with some religious overtones. If our only bond is Jesus Christ and life in Christ, we are a church—the body of Christ, the new community, God's new social order, the people of God.

## 1. *The Church Shares a Common Life in Christ*

Let your attitudes toward one another come from Jesus Christ and your life in him (see Phil. 2:5). "When Christ, who is our life, is revealed, then you also will be revealed with Him in glory" (Col. 3:4, NASB). From the viewpoint of our life in Christ, the only difference between the best Christian in the church and the worst sinner in the world is Jesus Christ. We come together as sinners who have life only in him. We do not live as believers because we ate bread yesterday. We live because of his life in us. People in the church are no longer prostitutes, thieves, conniving crooked politicians, greedy and ambition-oriented executives. People in the church no longer believe in the dog-eat-dog rat race going on in the world. We are sinners saved by grace. We have life in Christ. It is this life that we learn to share with one another. We take off our masks of hypocrisy. We wash off the veneer of culture. We are honest about ourselves with others. Now that we know who we are, the sham is no longer necessary. We share our common struggle to live our faith. The whole point of the great passage in the second chapter of Philippians is the need we have for the unselfish mind of Christ. There is great need for us to share our journey in Christ, both failures and successes, with our fellow travelers. It is from this sharing of life that we gain strength, compassion, and joy.

### 2. The Church Shares a Common Faith

In the early church described in Acts 2:42, the ones who believed shared their common life together. The Christians are called "believers" many times in our New Testament (Acts 5:14). The church is a people who have opened up their lives to God in Jesus Christ. The point here is not so much what they believed but the fact that they lived by faith. In fact, there is very little in the conversations of our Lord on faith as a body of beliefs. However, there is a great deal of emphasis on the life of faith. The faith shared by a congregation cannot be measured by the size of its mortgage on its beautiful new buildings. It is the faith shared that God will do what is best for the couple whose young child is retarded. It is the faith shared with the divorcee that God will bring something good and beautiful out of discarded dreams and a wrecked life. It is faith shared that the alcoholic notorious can become the alcoholic victorious. It is the faith shared that the compulsive liar's or gambler's shackles of habit can be broken. It is the faith shared that the heart attack or the cancer is not God's last word. The church is not prepared to share its faith with the world if it has never learned to share faith among the people of God. The church is even called "the household of faith" (Gal. 6:10). Paul calls Titus "my true child in a common faith" (Titus 1:4, NASB). Faith in God produces faith in people. Evangelism is faith in God to convict and convert. It is faith in people to respond to God's love. The Christian is never a cynic about God or people.

### 3. The Church Shares a Common Sinfulness

The church is a fellowship of sinners. It is so easy to fall into the trap of thinking that the sinners are "out there." The early church didn't turn people out for being sinners. It is true that some renounced their faith and left the church. The church did not leave them. Jesus said to treat an erring brother who persists in evil as "a Gentile and a tax-gatherer" (Matt. 18:17, NASB). But how did he treat Gentiles and tax gatherers? He ate with tax collectors. He loved and ministered to Gentiles. All of us agree that homes where children feel free to come to a parent and say, "Daddy,

I did a terrible thing . . . I know it was wrong . . . I don't know why I did it," are in much better shape than those where the children are afraid to talk about their mistakes and wrongdoing. The church needs a confessional. It needs to begin in the pulpit. It might begin a revival for a pastor to say, "This morning, fellow sinners, I don't have a message from God. I have been lazy. I didn't study. I didn't pray. I have been too busy doing other things. If you will pray for me, I will come back next week with my heart and head ready." That just might move some deacon to come and say, "Pastor, I am going through hell. I am being tempted by a young woman in my office. I am on the verge of throwing my family and everything overboard. I know I shouldn't do it. Pray for me that I will be strong and do the right thing." We can never learn how to deal with sinners "out there" with compassion and understanding until we learn to deal with sinners "in here" with compassion and understanding. In fact, we cannot deal with the sins of others until we have been honest about our own sins.

### 4. *The Church Shares a Common Burden*

Because the church is a body, when any part of the body is hurting the whole body is affected. "Bear one another's burdens, and thus fulfill the law of Christ" (Gal. 6:2, NASB). In this same passage (Gal. 6:5) we are commanded to carry our own load. In the fifth verse, the apostle emphasized the need for every person to bear his own burden. The second verse deals with our hurts and a mutual sharing of concerns.

"My husband told me last night he is getting a divorce."

"The doctor says it is carcinoma of the liver."

"Our only boy was picked up by the police for possession of hard drugs."

"Sarah told us last night she is pregnant."

"They are going to lay off five hundred men, and I may be one of them."

"The company asked me to take early retirement."

We are all human. Hurt us and we cry. Please us and we laugh. We find it so difficult to share our humanity.

In a renewal group of denominational and church leaders, one person opened up and shared some deep hurts with the group. He broke down and wept. One by one we began to share our common hurts. Every person in that room that night was hurting.

By the end of the session all of us began to take heart. We were not alone.

A pastor was broken-hearted by his son who got into drugs and finally committed a crime. The pastor tried to preach and couldn't. He then told the congregation the whole situation. The entire attitude of the congregation was changed toward him. All of a sudden he had joined the human race. Except for a very small group, the church rallied to his support. The burdened pastor discovered a new relationship with his church.

Good evangelism is listening to people who hurt. If we have not learned to listen to our fellow Christians, we cannot expect to be good listeners to hurting people outside the church.

### 5. The Church Shares a Common Love

One of the greatest gifts of Christ is the gift of his love. "This is My commandment, that you love one another, just as I have loved you (John 15:12, NASB). It is important that we realize the unique ways Christ loves us. His riches meet our poverty needs; his sinless life atones for our sinfulness; his strength provides for our weakness. He comes to us just as we are and offers us all that he has. When we open ourselves to him, he takes us just as we are. The body of Christ is to have that kind of love in its relationships with one another.

During a revival week, the pastor and I were visting some homes in the area. We visited one home where there was obvious financial, moral, and spiritual need. The woman was a divorcee with several children. There was dirt, neglect, and poverty. When we left the home the pastor said, "Oh, I do wish we could reach that family. There is so much we can do for them." This really was the love of Christ reaching out from plentitude to poverty. Until we learn how to love one another like that, we will not be able to love lost persons. John puts it very simply and very powerfully. "The one who does not love does not know God, for God is love" (1 John 4:8, NASB).

### 6. The Church Shares a Common Failure

Why does the church all too often fail to reflect this sharing?

1) *Because our organization and activity replaces the shared life.*—Sometimes it is because we allow activity and organization to subtly replace the shared life. Organization is certainly biblical. The New

Testament tells us how the early church organized itself. The church in the New Testament was engaged in many activities. The church can, however, find itself offering to each other and to outsiders the activity and the organization instead of the life. We constantly are inviting people to Sunday School, Church Training, WMU and Brotherhood meetings, or to socials and other events. We may do this with very little thought about the life in Christ we have to share. Sometimes there is no opportunity in these activities and organizations to touch each other, to share our selves and our needs, to really know one another. It may seem that the goal of the church has become growing organizations instead of growing persons in Christ. There is a need for organization, and we must not "shoot the dog to kill the fleas." The church must deal with both the individual and the group. Because it deals with the group, it needs organization. But the organization must not become "the whole bag." If it does, the individual and the sharing of life on a one-to-one basis will be lost. For an interesting and biblical discussion of this topic, I recommend chapter 1 of Lawrence O. Richards' book, *A Theology of Christian Education* (Zondervan, 1975).

2) *Because we belong for the wrong reasons.* —The church fails to reflect sharing because all too often our reasons for belonging to the church are for reasons other than our common faith. We have defined this faith as being open to Jesus Christ—to his lordship. The faith too often is a faith of the mind. It is a system of beliefs. Such a church is always ready for joyless and often caustic debate. It thrives and keeps alive by exposing the enemies of what its members believe. This kind of church attracts many persons in an aggressive (and often violent) society. Such a church spends most of its time exposing the error and "evil" in other Christian groups, and moves heaven and earth to "make one proselyte."

3) *Because we find our commonality in culture rather than Christ.* — Sometimes churches are people worshiping together because they are comfortable with one another. They find their commonality in their economic position, their rural heritage, or the color of their skin. The church that shares its faith is a church that finds one point of commonality—Jesus Christ. We may be very diverse racially, socially, and economically, but the overriding point of contact and touch is our faith in Jesus Christ as Lord. The church is the called-out people of God. They are called out from Jew and Gentile to become the new race of men, the new social order—the church.

This is the faith that binds us together. This is the faith we share. We must share our faith with one another before we can share it with the world. We are long on exhortations about love but short on demonstration.

4) *Because of our neglect.*—Another reason that we fail at the point of being a sharing church is that our own people fail to see very much self-effacing love in our relationships with one another. A church made up of uptight people who cannot tolerate others who are different is not a community of shared love. A church whose reputation in the community is gained by luxurious buildings and efficient organizations is not a community of shared love. The church that has an official or unofficial ban on people because of the color of their skin is not a community of shared love. When we want our members to conform to our ideas of "what our kind of people are like," we are not a community of shared love. Many of our churches (and especially the larger ones) are full of lonely, neglected people who need a ministry in Christian love. They may be retired people, old and ill, who no longer can attend services. Some of them have not been personally visited by members of their church in years. Anyone who has conducted a radio or television ministry can discover this from letters that are received. In the church and in marriage the words "I love you" can be cheap, but acts of loving concern are costly and hard to come by.

5) *Because of our failure to share in the task.*—Underlying our lack of love is our failure to share burdens, both the heart kind and the work kind. In most churches a few people carry most of the work load. Is this an indication of love? Each of us is to help carry the others' heart burdens. Each of us is to carry his share of the work burden. Do we love one another if we allow one person to be a burden bearer while we freeload on the congregation?

6) *Because people are not free to be themselves.*—The result of this failure in sharing is that we do not allow people the freedom to be what they are. Instead we have a tendency to force people into established molds according to traditions. This more than anything else explains an unhealthy clique often found within the church. There may be a small group of conformists at the center who control things and a much larger group on the periphery who are unwilling to conform. The core group may wonder why the others are "not faithful." The core group may not even know that they are unconsciously asking everyone to be like them. Everyone is expected

We often fail in being a sharing church because of neglect. Many of our churches are full of lonely, neglected people who are old and ill and in need of ministry.

to attend everything, whether it appeals to them or was designed to meet their needs. In order to be a "good member," one must do what everyone else does. There is very little adjustment made for cultural differences, for intellectual levels, and for personal gifts. There is very little effort expended to accept people as they are. So many people have a sign hanging on them that cannot be seen. It says, "Love me for heaven's sake; God is not through with me yet." How can we ever become open enough to touch with love and compassion persons whose life-styles threaten us? Our circle of love must be big enough to include youth with long hair, persons with a different skin color, social reformers, and others who are different from us.

## III. What the Evangelistic Church Does

The church is the medium for communicating the message. The message concerns how God has met the need of sinful man in Jesus Christ. He is "the Christ, the Son of the living God" (Matt. 16:16). On the foundation rock of that testimony, Christ builds his church. In giving the church that message, he has given the church the "keys to the kingdom of heaven" (see Matt. 16:16-19). The church is not to decide what the message is. The message has been given to us. We are not to be concerned about the shape of the message; we are to be concerned about communicating it. It is the message of life and death.

On the other hand, the church is not a tape recorder into which the Lord dictates the message so that it always comes out the same. The message is always shaped and colored by the mind, the emotions, and the will of the medium. This is the way God wants it to be. He made us all different. Depending on the medium, there are different kinds of appeals, some more emotional, some more intellectual, and some more appealing to the will. But the message is the same: *Jesus Christ is Lord.*

America has been evangelized to a greater degree than any nation is history because its evangelism has been as varied as its people. There are formal churches and informal churches, established churches and free churches, house churches and cathedral churches, wealthy churches and people's churches. Wherever a church is a medium for communicating the message that *Jesus Christ is Lord*, it is a church being used of God. In order to effectively communicate the gospel, the church must do certain biblical things well. They are the things that Jesus did.

### 1. The Evangelistic Church Proclaims

To use more familiar terminology, the church preaches. The church preaches the biblical truth about God, man, Jesus Christ, and judgment. In the sixties, there was a rediscovery of the laity which is (thank God) still with us. In the seventies, there is a rediscovery of preaching. The numbers and the quality of seminary students are ample testimony to this. In the sixties many pastors were trying to get out of preaching. Now hundreds of youth are knocking on our door to get into preaching. In the sixties, pessimistic apostles of doom were proclaiming the death of preaching. Today preaching has come into its own. The proclamation of the Word is central to the life and work of the church. What we discovered in the critical years of the sixties and the revival years of the seventies is that the church and each member of the church is responsible for proclamation.

The Word of God, preached by a man who preaches for today and zeroes in on the totality of life, has never been more needed or more well received. People are interested in what the Bible says. Expository preaching that has a theme and a simple, easily remembered outline that comes directly from the context of Scripture is "in" with the people of God. The new emphasis on the layperson as a minister is no threat to the ordained, trained preacher. There are many places where the lay preacher is needed. He can go to places where the voice of the pastor is never heard. The pastor's message needs to be repeated over and over again by laypersons in shops, factories, business establishments, commuter trains, airliners, and city streets. When persecution drove the laypersons out of Jerusalem, they went everywhere preaching the word while the apostles remained in Jerusalem (Acts 8:1-5). Jesus himself was a preacher of the word (Mark 1:14). He preached the greatest sermon ever delivered (Matt. 5—7).

### 2. The Evangelistic Church Teaches

Jesus Christ was a teacher. "And He began again to teach by the seashore" (Mark 4:1, NASB). Jesus was a master of teaching. He delivered very few lectures. The great sermon that Jesus delivered on the mountain was called teaching (Matt. 5:2). When Paul listed the gifts of Christ to church leaders, he listed the pastor-teacher. No preaching is worth our time that does not teach. Christian education today is largely limited to classroom teaching. The church teaches by parables, models, dramatic bits of life, group dynamics, and one-to-one discipling, as well as the classroom. When the church in a business meeting debated hotly whether or not to receive blacks, was it teaching? When the church in business meeting voted to cut missions 5 percent in order to meet mortgage payments, was it teaching? When the pastor resigned because he didn't get his way about something, was he teaching? A church or an individual may teach the wrong things by careless actions.

The teaching that the church does is much too content-oriented and too little action-oriented. Just because we teach the Bible does not mean that its teachings become a part of our life and living. There are certain things that cannot be taught by an authority figure standing up and telling people about it. Discipleship and ministry must be parabled and modeled in life-styles. Teaching must be demonstration as well as exhortation. Some teachers often are poorly prepared and poor models for what they are teaching. They may have been chosen in order to fill out the organization. Little attention was given to their qualifications as evangelistic models in discipleship and ministry. Church groups need to be involved in actually doing ministry and in discipling others. It is a cliché but it is true: I would rather see a sermon than hear one any day.

### 3. The Evangelistic Church "Disciples"

This is the word consistently used in the four Gospels to describe the relationship between the Lord and his followers. It is interesting to know that the word is not used in the Epistles at all. There may be a link, however, in the angelic instruction to "go, tell His disciples and Peter . . ." (Mark 16:7, NASB). In the commission in Matthew, the church is given a mandate "to make disciples" (28:19). Discipling is a proper part of preaching and teaching. However, one of the reasons we have neglected the cultivation of personal relationships with Jesus Christ is that we have not really seen discipling as a definite part of what the church is to do. Pastors often are so involved in the church mechanics that they have no time to be disciples of Jesus Christ. The disciple has a priority loyalty to Jesus Christ. He belongs to Jesus Christ. His commitment to follow Jesus Christ takes priority over his commitment to home, job, and self-interest (Luke 14:26-27,33). Some youth have rediscovered "discipleship" in many of the para-church groups. This began with groups such as the "Jesus people" in the sixties. They discovered something that had been neglected in many of the organized churches. There are many church leaders who cannot see a difference in being a disciple and being a "good church member." A person can be a good churchman without being a real disciple of Jesus Christ. The evangelistic church needs to discover ways that it can provide content and models for making disciples.

Since discipleship involves a personal relationship with a person, it is not something that can be acquired through "content" teaching alone. It is demonstrated, parabled, and infectiously caught. It involves prayer, study of the Word, knowing the person and work of the Holy Spirit, growth in personal devotion to Jesus Christ, and cultivating Christlike graces in personal relationships.

### 4. The Evangelistic Church Ministers

Jesus announced that he came into the world to minister and to die (Mark 10:45). If the church is on his mission, then it must know how to minister. Paul considered himself a minister. The deacons were appointed to minister. "Minister" is one of the great words of the New Testament. It cannot be neglected in any consideration of what the church is to do. In the mind of Christ, ministry is to be the last word as to how it goes with us in the judgment. The question will not simply be, "Were you orthodox in your faith?" The question will be ours, and we will ask, "When did we see you naked, Lord, and fail to clothe you?" (see Matt. 25:31-46). The criterion of our judgment will be ministry.

If we are like Jesus, we will minister. Ministry has an authenticating power for the gospel and the church. Jesus affirmed persons in their need. The evangelistic church cannot "pass by on the other side." Because Jesus ministered to people, great crowds followed him. He was meeting their need. It was not his sermons that attracted persons. Indeed, quite often his words were offensive to people. Churches that begin to meet the needs of people soon discover that the news is too good to keep. The word is soon out that the church is a caring church with people who know how to love and be loved for Christ's sake. All around us are the infected sores of society. What is our healing, reconciling word? Are we following Jesus in ministry?

## Review

The mission of the church in the world is the mission of Jesus Christ. When we discover why he came, we know what the church is to do in the world. The church communicates its message by what it does as well as by what it says. Often there is a credibility gap between what the church says and what it does. The evangelistic church is a sharing church. Churches that have never learned how to share with one another will have difficulty in sharing the gospel with non-Christians. The church shares its common life in Christ, its common faith, its common burdens, its common sinfulness, and its common love. Sometimes the activity and organization are allowed to substitute for the shared life. The church can find itself offering to outsiders the organizational life of the church rather than life in Christ. The church often is guilty of talking about love instead of actually "fleshing out" his love.

The church not only is, but it does. What the church does grows out of what the church is. The church proclaims. The word of God preached by a man who preaches for today and zeroes in on the totality of life has never been more needed or more well received. The emphasis on the layperson as a minister does not detract from the leadership, preaching, and equipping role of the pastor-teacher. The church teaches. The teaching of the church needs to be less content-oriented and more action-oriented. The church "disciples." The word "disciple" and the word "equip" are different words for the same process of preparing persons for effective ministry. Jesus came to minister. The evangelistic church ministers.

## Questions for Discussion

1. In the introduction to chapter 2, the author gives four purposes for Christ's coming into the world, supported by four statements of Christ. How is the mission of the church related to these four passages?
2. Do we really think it would be helpful if we were honest with one another about our sins?
3. What are some of the reasons we have for belonging to the

church? How valid are our reasons in the light of the discussion in chapter 2?

4. How can laypersons be preachers of the Word of God?

5. How important is ministry in the mind of the author? Do you feel that ministry is that important in the life of the church?

# CHAPTER 3

I. A Theology of Opportunity
   1. The Transformation of Zaccheus
   2. Who Is Jesus?
   3. Zaccheus Found Himself
II. A Theology of Involvement
   1. The Call to Discipleship Is a Call to Involvement
   2. How We Can Become Involved with People
   3. Ministering to Persons with Variant Life-styles
   4. The Church Must Be Deliberately Open to People of All Kinds
   5. Persons with Whom We Can Become Involved
III. A Theology of Incarnation
   1. God Was Incarnate in Jesus Christ
   2. Incarnating Christ in Discipleship
IV. A Theology of Liberation
   1. What Freedom in Christ Is Like
   2. Jesus Christ Preached Liberation
   3. Only Free People Can Proclaim Freedom
V. A Theology of Hope
   1. Hope in Christ Is Hope for Today
   2. Hope in Christ Is Hope for the World

# 3
# A Theology for an
# Evangelistic Church

Robert Raines, in his book *Creative Brooding,* quotes from one of Herb Gardner's plays. Murray is in his thirties, out of work, and responsible for the care of his nephew. A social worker comes to take Norman, the nephew, away from Murray because he is an unfit guardian for the boy. Murray says to the social worker, ". . . I just want him to stay with me till I can be sure he won't turn into *Norman Nothing.* I want to be sure he'll know when he's chickening out on himself. I want him to know exactly the special thing he is or else he won't notice it when it starts to go. I want him to stay awake and know who the phonies are. . . . And I want him to know the subtle, sneaky, important reason why he was born a human being and not a chair." [1]

## I. A Theology of Opportunity

Jesus met a man in Jericho and went home with him so that he would not be a Zaccheus Nothing.

> *And He entered and was passing through Jericho. And behold, there was a man called by the name of Zaccheus; and he was a chief tax-gatherer, and he was rich. And he was trying to see who Jesus was, and he was unable because of the crowd, for he was small in stature. And he ran on ahead and climbed up into a sycamore tree in order to see Him, for He was about to pass through that way. And when Jesus came to the place, He looked up and said to him, "Zaccheus, hurry and come down, for today I must stay at your house." And he hurried and came down,*

45

*and received Him gladly. And when they saw it, they all began to grumble, saying, "He has gone to be the guest of a man who is a sinner." And Zaccheus stopped and said to the Lord, "Behold, Lord, half of my possessions I will give to the poor, and if I have defrauded anyone of anything, I will give back four times as much." And Jesus said to him, "Today salvation has come to this house, because he, too, is a son of Abraham. For the Son of Man has come to seek and to save that which was lost" (Luke 19:1-10, NASB).*

## 1. The Transformation of Zaccheus

Jesus used the occasion of Zaccheus' conversion to make one of the three announcements of his mission after Caesarea Philippi. He came into the world to help persons find God and find themselves (v. 10). He came into the world to save them from their lostness. He came to help persons who do not know where they are, or who they are. He came to reveal who God is and God's love for sinners. He came to help us find ourselves in our lostness. It is interesting to note that Zaccheus not only wanted to see Jesus, but he wanted to see "who Jesus was."

## 2. Who Is Jesus?

Jesus Christ has many names, and in the names an answer can be found as to just how we are to know him. He is Jesus and this name indicated his relationship to the world. He is the Jesus of history. He is the one who divided time by his birth in Bethlehem's manger. This is all that the pagans know about him. He is Jesus, "the Christ." The term "Christ" is simply the Greek meaning for the Jewish "Messiah." This term refers to his relationship to the Jews, that covenant people of promise. He is "Son of God," and this name tells us his relationship to the Father. He is "God of very God." Our knowledge of God is wrapped up in human flesh and blood. He is Savior, and this name reveals his relationship to sinners. He came into the world to save men from their lostness. He is Lord, and this name reveals his relationship to the church. He is Lord of the church and Lord of every believer. There is no way to know him as Savior and not know him as Lord. The saving confession is "Jesus Christ is Lord." On the day that changed his life, Zaccheus knew he had entertained no ordinary person as his guest.

The church may not be sure of everything, but it must be sure of who Jesus Christ is. There can be no vacillating here. By the miracle of his birth, by the stainless purity of his life, by the transforming power of his death, by the mighty power of his bodily resurrection, he is declared "with power to be the Son of God" (Rom. 1:4, NASB). Jesus at Caesarea Philippi asks the burning question to be answered by the church, "Who are you saying that I am?" The church that hesitates over the deity of Jesus Christ cannot be evangelistic.

The proclamation of the Word is the Word that "was God . . . was in the beginning with God . . . apart from Him nothing came into being that has come into being" (John 1:1-3, NASB). The proclamation of the Word is the proclamation of "the word of the cross" (1 Cor. 1:18, NASB). The Word was the Son of God creating in the beginning. The Word was the Son of God dying on the Cross. The Word of God acting in creation brought order out of chaos. The Word of God acting in atoning death brought life out of death. Zaccheus came to know someone who so utterly changed his life that he was no longer the same man. The church proclaims the Word. This function of the church must never be downgraded or undercut by anything. The proclamation is the good news of what God has done in his mighty acts in Jesus Christ.

### 3. Zaccheus Found Himself

Humanity suffers from an identity crisis. As Bonhoeffer pointed out, man sees himself as having no beginning and no end. He is literally, in the terms of the world, "behind the eight ball." For Zaccheus, there was only the greedy, grasping present; and success was determined by how many bloody dollars he had at the end of the day.

Then Zaccheus found God in Jesus Christ. He also found himself that day long ago. He found out that he was not just a moneybag but a man made in the image of God. He found that there is more to live for than just accumulating things.

Without God in Jesus Christ, who is "Alpha and Omega, the beginning and the end," a person has no hard answers to the question of his being. When he finds himself in the God who is the beginning and the end, he knows who he is, why he is here, and where he is going. Only then does he discover a genesis and a revelation. There really are no options for a person without

nto life. For a terminus,
ness and despair are the
nooses to wear in a life
Jesus came to seek and
rch of Jesus Christ must

discovered their identity
neir life upon this planet
e lost. The blind cannot
s for the deaf. Zaccheus'
lted in a growing under-
d struggled so frantically
had to be given away.
in constant grasping for
king lots, ornate fixtures,
cumulation of things. In
esus said, "Do not worry
ed colors. I take care of
tly about what you are
e care of you" (see Matt.
come living footnotes to
an in proper perspective
subtle, sneaky, important
s and not chairs.

with Zaccheus. Zaccheus
le "played ball" with the
countrymen for gain. He
"Publicans and sinners"
get the foulness off their
pat on the ground. Jesus
oing home with Zaccheus
the religious sensibilities
n a strict diet of segrega-
Jesus was involved with
the lepers, were sinners
t; but Jesus even touched
ics and "seizure people"

were declared taboo by the Jewish religious teachers, but Jesus got involved with them. Even in Christ's death, he made a choice to die between two thieves. Jesus' involvement with sinners more than anything else aroused the resentment, animosity, and finally the hatred of the religious leaders.

1. *Discipleship Is a Call to Involvement*
Involvement is clearly evident in the experience of the first disciples. When persons enrolled in the school of Christ, their first lesson was a lesson in involvement. They brought the sick, the palsied, the lame, the epileptics, and even the lepers to Jesus. He let the disciples see the writhing bodies, the foaming mouths, the twisted limbs, and the ulcerated running sores. Jesus wanted the disciples to see and feel with his same kind of compassionate care. After being criticized about his involvement with the undesirables, Jesus said, "I did not come to call the righteous, but sinners to repentance" (Matt. 9:13). He said that people who are well do not need a doctor, but those who are sick (Matt. 9:12). We walk by, sit by, fly by, pass by, and work by persons every day who are hurting. Jesus calls us to get involved. It might help us to pray a prayer framed for us by Robert Raines in *Creative Brooding*:

> *I stand in the window and watch most of the time,*
> *and admire Jesus Christ from a distance,*
> *a safe distance.*
> *I like to take things easy and enjoy life, Lord.*
> *Am I a fool?*
> *Why does that phrase "what do I care?" bother me?*
> *I do care about justice in this country,*
> *and happiness in my family,*
> *and faith in you, Lord.*
>
> *Make me care enough to commit myself,*
> *and get involved.*[2]

2. *Getting Involved with People*
There is no need for us to say, "I do not know what to do." Hospitals, jails, mental institutions, prison rehabilitation units, work with troubled teenagers—all are crying for volunteers to minister to people who are in need. What an opportunity for Christian testimony and Christlike living! A state director of work with

nonreaders, who is an outstanding Christian, said recently, "I am using materials put out by the American Bible Society to teach nonreaders. I thought by using these materials and by appealing to churches, I would have more help than I could use. After some months not one church in my own denomination (Southern Baptist) has volunteered to help." No one wanted to get involved. There are materials available to any church who desires to get involved with alcoholics, drug users, nonreaders, and other similar groups. Such materials are available from both denominational and governmental agencies.

### 3. *Ministering to Persons with Variant Life-styles*

Jesus was open not only to people who were hurting but also to persons with variant life-styles. Zaccheus was a case in point. He was hated by both the Romans and the Jews. He was living in a "no man's land" of nonacceptance. Today there are thousands of persons in the vicinity of our churches whose life-styles are different from ours. This variance represents an insurmountable barrier to church-oriented persons unless our lives are patterned after the Man from Galilee. For instance, three divorcee mothers with five children may share a large apartment. One mother takes care of the children while the other two work and support the combined families. Their life-style is so different that it is difficult for the church to minister to them. The church may minister to homes only in the context of the "orthodox" concept of the home. We have persons whose life-styles are different from us that need Christ's redemptive ministry. Our churches should communicate compassion and care for them, as Christ did to all persons.

Jesus never condoned sin, but he expressed love and acceptance for sinners. Most of the older denominations have slowly become upper-middle-class. They have lost their sensitivity to the poor. People living below the poverty level, receiving government assistance, are not comfortable in a situation where their life-style is regarded as immoral and patent evidence of laziness and slothfulness. Young married couples living on the thin edge of poverty, cheated of the privilege of decent housing because of high prices, might beat a path to the door of the church that would assist them in balancing their budget as well as "saving their souls."

Discipleship is a call to involvement. Needs are everywhere for Christian testimony and Christlike living. Working with nonreaders is one avenue of opportunity.

### 4. An Open Church to People of All Kinds

Left to normal sociological forces, the church becomes a thin slice of the population. People tend to group with their economic, racial, and cultural peers. One church may be a "people's" church and another an upper-middle-class church. If a church is to be pluralistic in its evangelism, it must plan to do it. The first step in such planning is a determination to be open to another group of persons who are "different" in language, life-style, or culture. An old church in a declining community may have a middle-class congregation who has moved out of the community but still comes to the old church because of traditional ties. The church may now be surrounded with laboring people. If the church communicates an anti-labor attitude these persons will not be reached. This pluralism is a must for the inner-city church. Rural churches and city churches often die when they cannot be open to a new situation with new demands in a rapidly changing life and life-style in America. Almost all of our churches are surrounded by pockets of people who are different, whom Christ loves, and whom we have an obligation to evangelize.

### 5. Persons with Whom We Can Be Involved

The church in planning for evangelism needs to ask the question, "Are there persons and groups of persons in our community with whom we have little or no communication?" Then ask another question equally important, "Do we have a responsibility to evangelize these persons?" What we are really saying is that Jesus did not draw lines of distinction in determining the target groups for his evangelism. If the evangelism of the church is the evangelism of Jesus, we will get involved with persons of all kinds and types. In most cases Jesus ministered to people and touched their lives with his life-changing forces. Singles who have a need for Christian fellowship with their peer group will come to the church that ministers to that need. Divorcees need love and acceptance. They will attend the church that ministers to them. Poor people have a need for a feeling of dignity and purpose. They will come to the church that ministers to that need. Lonely senior citizens have a need at the point of fellowship and personal fulfillment. They will come to the church that meets that need. Jesus ministered to the deepest needs of people because he loved them. He did not ask if they were rich or poor, sinful or righteous. He met their needs. In meeting their needs they came in contact with the power of his life. Christians and churches must get involved.

## III. A Theology of Incarnation

God was incarnate in Jesus Christ. This is the "mystery of godliness, Christ . . . manifest in the flesh" (1 Tim. 3:16). Christ is manifested in the life of the church which is his body (Eph. 1:22-23). Upon his encounter with Jesus Christ, Zaccheus gave away his money to the poor. He made restitution for the wrongs he had done four times over. Something happened to him that made him a Jesus person.

### 1. God Was Incarnate in Jesus Christ

The fact of the incarnation is celebrated by Christians in worship each Sunday and occupies a special season of the year we call Christmas. If we take John 17:21 seriously, it was the God of eternity, of creation, of revelation and salvation who came to eat with Zaccheus that day. We also believe from this passage that when the believer gets involved with the lost, like Zaccheus, and begins to parabolize and verbalize the Way, then the believer is incarnating that very God. What we celebrate in the lost person finding God and finding himself is that God in Christ has come to live in that person. He will never be the same.

This process of growing Christlikeness is called discipleship in the Gospels. The relationship between disciple and Master, between pupil and Teacher comes to be close and so real that the disciple-pupil begins to take on the characteristics and the life-style of the Master-Teacher. For many years at Southwestern Seminary, L. R. Scarborough so influenced his students in his evangelism classes that many of them unconsciously adopted his facial expressions and body language. It is this kind of relationship that the disciples had to Jesus. The matter of our personal relationship and commitment to Jesus Christ has not been emphasized as much as it needs to be in the preaching and teaching of the church. The emphasis in our preaching and teaching usually is on being good church persons, and this is needful. If the lives of believers are to become living footnotes to the gospel, there needs to be a new emphasis on personal devotion to Jesus Christ. Upon our conversion, Jesus Christ comes to live in us and we live in him

(Eph. 2:13). This work of the grace of God—being in Christ and Christ in us—has taken place in the very center of our lives. What God has worked in us must be worked out by us (Phil. 2:12-13). The first is possession by relationship to Christ. The second is a process which is related to learning and doing. That learning and doing is discipleship. Paul calls it "fruitful labor" (Phil. 1:22, NASB).

### 2. Incarnating Christ in Discipleship

With his own life as the supreme example, Jesus calls us to discipleship—incarnating his life in us. In Luke 14 a large crowd was following him (v. 25). He turned to them and threw out a challenge to discipleship. What we have in this passage is three pivotal conditions for the life of incarnating Christ.

The disciple cannot be possessed by others (v. 26). The disciple belongs to Jesus Christ and not to loved ones, a corporation, or his work. There are many Christians who could be effective witnesses as disciples, but they allow work to keep them from complete commitment to Christ. A pastor could conceivably be so "owned" by a church that he has no time to be Christ's disciple.

A disciple cannot be possessed by self (v. 27). Jesus does not ask us to bear his cross, but *ours*. This is the cross of self-denial. Some persons, like Zaccheus, are overambitious to make money or move up the ladder of corporate success. Subsequently they have no time for personal discipleship. Time studies, sales charts, and management courses may take the place of our Bibles for daily reading. Disciples cannot be possessed by things (v. 33). This was the primary problem with Zaccheus. He seemed to realize that Christian discipleship had some price tags on it. The grace of God is free, but it is never cheap. Incarnating Christ in Christian discipleship is not an easy thing to be undertaken lightly (vv. 28-33).

## IV. A Theology of Liberation

Zaccheus found a freedom in Jesus Christ that he had never known. He discovered freedom from the tyranny of others, of self, of things.

### 1. What Freedom in Christ Is Like

Zaccheus was a slave of the Romans, even though well rewarded.

He was in bondage to his own greedy ambitions. He was possessed by money and the power that it made him feel. He knew what it meant to walk down the street with sweaty palms and feel the hatred that exuded from everyone he met. The Jews hated him, and the Romans despised him. He was even a slave to that growing pile of gold he had accumulated. In many ways Zaccheus was like Dickens' Scrooge. Scrooge flung open the window after his visit from the ghost of Christmas future and began to cry out "Merry Christmas" to a brand new world. The beneficent visit of Scrooge to the home of Tiny Tim reminds us of the visits (which we can easily imagine) of Zaccheus to the homes of those he cheated. For both Scrooge and Zaccheus it was a liberating experience that brought them to themselves and set them free.

### 2. Jesus Christ Preached Liberation

There is great emphasis on liberation in what Jesus says to us. He says that men are slaves to sin. He tells us that there is real liberation to be found in his sayings (words) (John 8:34-37). Referring to his great sermon, Christ is saying that happiness (freedom) is found in being merciful, pure in heart, gentle, and peacemaking (Matt. 5:1-10). The Jews said to him in John 8, "Why do you talk to us about being free? We have never been slaves to anyone" (see v. 33). Had they forgotten their bondage in Egypt? Did they fail to see that at that very moment the hated Romans were occupying their land? It is the very nature of sin that the slave thinks he is free. The alcoholic will insist that Christians are not free because they do not feel free to drink. He fails to see his own slavery to the bottle.

### 3. Only Free People Can Proclaim Freedom

The Sermon on the Mount is about attitudes. Christ changes the way we see things. This new attitude sets us free. The drug addict insists that he can "kick it" anytime. The sensualist insists that his obsession with sex is normal. The racist insists that he "really likes those people." It is not until we feel Christ's liberating love that we see the shackles that bind us. It is this "new attitude" that causes us to recoil in horror from the former things we loved, defended, and enjoyed while they were enslaving us. For the Christian, freedom is the freedom to say no to the evil and yes to the good.

Many of our churches are surrounded by pockets of
people who are different, whom Christ loves and
whom we have an obligation to evangelize.

Our most pressing problem in communicating a gospel of liberation is that many church members do not transmit liberation. When Christians are the captives of ideas, cultural hang-ups, attitudes, and are even slaves to vicious habits, they are not likely to be liberators. The world cries with justification, "Physician, heal thyself" (Luke 4:23). It is difficult for us to communicate love out of racist attitudes. It is difficult for us to communicate liberation when we are not really free from those demonic powers, carnal appetites, and destructive attitudes that enslave us. Paul warned the Galatians about becomeing slaves again even after being set free. "It was for freedom that Christ set us free; therefore keep standing firm and do not be subject again to a yoke of slavery" (Gal. 5:1, NASB). "For you were called to freedom, brethren; only do not turn your freedom into an opportunity for the flesh, but through love serve one another" (Gal. 5:13, NASB). Paul urged the Galatians not to return to bondage or to a legalistic religion or to fleshly appetites. Only free persons can preach freedom and lead others to freedom. The evangelistic church is on a mission of liberation. It is a thrilling mission—to deliver those who are in bondage. When God in Jesus Christ strikes the shackles off the alcoholic, the drug addict, the racist, the money lover, and the sensualist, it is good to be there as a bearer of the message and sing with the liberated, "Free at last, free at last. Thank God, free at last."

## V. A Theology of Hope

For Zaccheus Nothing there is hope. For the world there is hope. For the evangelistic church there is hope.

### 1. Hope in Christ Is Hope for Today
If God in Jesus Christ can change one man, he can change all men. The Christian hope is not just hope in a redeemed society in the future where all things shall be brought under his administrative control (see Eph. 1:10, NASB). It is hope for today. People can be changed by the power of God.

### 2. Hope in Christ Is Hope for the World
Because people can be changed, society can be changed. The evangelistic church must never succumb to the pessimism that all

e is nothing that we can
rating love. We can live
lanations of the gospel.
s of persons to redeem

deemed, liberated, and
ething no one else can
r them and parable his
iged, his home can be
d, his profession can be
The evangelistic church
ne world. There is hope.
ll." He will do the rest.


man. He was a nothing.
from being a nothing.
esus Christ is. If we are
e sure about ourselves
evangelism is a theology
ne incarnation is God's
agedy of man's existence
will be involved with
will be open to persons
not condone sin, but he

uralistic. This pluralism
s tend to become people
ith one another. People
ten their traditions and
open to all persons, it
ercome the natural man
nself doing exactly what
noney. There is a process
ne believer. We actually
body. The theology of
ccheus was free from his
r relationship with Jesus
vith things. The church

preaches a liberating gospel and is on a mission of liberation.

## Questions for Discussion

1. The author makes a point of Zaccheus being in danger of being a nothing. Do you think that his description is an accurate picture of persons who are not Christians? Can we see some of these same characteristics in persons who are members of the church?
2. Is your church involved with persons and the life of the community?
3. Are there groups of persons in your community that are untouched by any of your church's ministries? Can you identify some of these groups?
4. What are some of the ways that Christians incarnate Jesus Christ? Do you think that most people would rather see a sermon than hear one?
5. In what ways are Christians free where others may be in bondage?

---

[1] From *A Thousand Clowns,* a play by Herb Gardner, © Copyright 1961, Random House, Inc.

[2] Reprinted with permission of Macmillan Publishing Co., Inc. from *Creative Brooding.* Copyright © Robert A. Raines, 1966.

# CHAPTER 4

I. The Purpose for Ministry
   1. What Others Are Saying About Life's Problems
   2. The Church Is in the World Arena to Minister
   3. The Ministry of the Layperson Is the Priesthood of the Believer in Action
II. The Equippers for Ministry
   1. The Gifts of Leadership for the Office-bearers of the Church
   2. The Pastor-Teacher's Evangelistic Ministry of Equipping
   3. The Pastor-Teacher Is an Administrator of the Church's Evangelistic Task
III. The Parables of Ministry
   1. The First Deacons' Ministry Role in the Church Is Our Example
   2. The Deacon's Role Is One of Ministry to the People of God
   3. The Deacon and "His Flock" Assist in Equipping for Ministry
IV. The Ministers of Ministry
   1. Christian Ministry Is Inseparable from "Evangelistic Ministry"
   2. Opportunities for Lay Ministry Abound in Our Communities
   3. The Vision of Jesus Is for Every Christian to Be a Minister

# 4

# The Evangelistic Church
# in Ministry

## I. The Purpose for Ministry

The church is in the world, but what in the world is it for? This question is still being asked in spite of the religious awakening that we have had since the advent of the seventies. There are increasing numbers of persons, including many of our youth, who are seeing the church as an anachronism with really nothing to say to life's real problems and nothing to do except to offer a religious pacifier to old people who are afraid to die. There are great evangelistic churches both large and small who are really saying something and saying it very well. Vibrant, living churches are attracting thousands of youth. They are feeding into our colleges and seminaries hundreds of youths who are committed to Christian callings. These churches, however, are few and far between when compared to the total number of churches and the total growing population.

### 1. What Others Are Saying About Life's Problems

There are those who are saying that all of life's problems can be solved in the laboratory of the scientist or on the couch of the psychiatrist. Truth and meaning for them are only things that can be tested by the five senses. This is called scientism. Others are saying that the real meaning of life is only in living this present moment. Squeeze what you can out of present existence because that is all there is. This is called atheistic existentialism. Another group is saying that the only real thing is human existence and personality. Persons have in themselves the possibility for good and greatness. They will ultimately triumph over what is bestial, primitive, and evil. This is called humanism. A fourth group depends on the other three. They are saying that there are no moral absolutes. What is right and good depends on the present situation. This view is sometimes called relativism. All of these views really see the supernatural—the Bible, God, Jesus Christ, miracles, and all religion—as a pious fraud.

Scientism is a dead-end street named disappointment. Existentialism is a dead-end street named despair. Humanism is a dead-end street named defeat. Relativism is a dead-end street named disgrace. Still they demand and receive the loyalty of millions of people in the United States. Many who believe some of these things still call themselves Christians. In all fairness we must say that some of the things they say about the church contain a great deal of truth. They say, "The church is unwilling to change even when truth is at stake." They point out that in one period of history the church refused to change and even persecuted people because they believed the sun to be the center of the universe. They also point out the unwillingness of the church to change nineteenth-century structures in a twentieth-century world. They say, "The church is insensitive to social issues." This has been true in many cases in the past. It is unfortunate that a generation of youth, sensitive to social justice, saw the church in the back seat rather than the driver's seat in the struggle for civil rights for minorities in the United States. Most evangelical churches were silent in regard to political and economic corruption in the sixties. Too often the church waited until the issues became popular before taking a stand.

### 2. The Church Is in the World Arena to Minister

What is the mission of the church? What in the world are we to do? It is clear that our task is to evangelize the mass of humanity who are caught up in and confused by many ideologies that have overturned many traditions and concepts. As stated in chapter 2, the mission of the church is the mission of Christ. It is to bring to fullness what Jesus came to do in the world. We are to do this by proclaiming Jesus Christ in the certainty that he is King and Servant. We confess that he is King by our obedience to his command. We confess that he is Servant by being the servant people—the servant church. In order to fulfill his mission, Christ

The church is in the world arena to minister. It is
clear that our task is to evangelize the masses of humanity who are caught up in and confused by many
ideologies that have overturned many traditions and
concepts.

called and discipled (empowered, equipped, and trained) persons to minister. He announced his mission as coming into the world not to be ministered to but to minister. The church in the book of Acts did very well in spite of the opposition of organized religion and philosophies. Our world is no more beset by ideologies than the world of the first century. The early church let "the world do their thing" while they "did their thing." "Their thing" won the day. They did it by being and proclaiming the gospel. They said, "What we are saying to you about Jesus Christ is true." Their lives were testimonies to the truth of their words. Priests and sinners, slaves and masters, rich and poor, intellectuals and the ignorant, Jews and Gentiles—all became part of the new society of God. How "they loved one another" was its own advertisement.

The church is in the arena. The teachings of the New Testament are clear. We are in conflict. Our only weapon is Christ's love, and our only word is faith. When Norway was occupied by the Nazis and beset by their obscenities, the Bishop of Norway said, "There is a foe; there is a fight; there is a faith." The apostle Paul expressed similar thoughts when he wrote:

> Finally, be strong in the Lord, and in the strength of His might. Put on the full armor of God, that you may be able to stand firm against the schemes of the devil. For our struggle is not against flesh and blood, but against the rulers, against the powers, against the world-forces of this darkness, against the spiritual forces of wickedness in the heavenly places. Therefore, take up the full armor of God, that you may be able to resist in the evil day, and having done everything, to stand firm. Stand firm therefore, having girded your loins with truth, and having put on the breastplate of righteousness, and having shod your feet with the preparation of the gospel of peace; in addition to all, taking up the shield of faith with which you will be able to extinguish all the flaming missiles of the evil one. And take the helmet of salvation, and the sword of the Spirit, which is the word of God. With all prayer and petition pray at all times in the Spirit, and with this in view, be on the alert with all perseverance and petition for all the saints (Eph. 6:10-18, NASB).

The church must answer every criticism of unbelief with loving, Christlike ministry. We do not retaliate by answering argument with argument. We must become involved with hurting humanity. But our involvement must not be just to "outdo" false ideas with "good works." We must become involved because we are impelled by Christ's love to love the unlovely and "to do good to those who speak all manner of evil against us." When false faiths rail against us, we must correct those things that they are saying about us that are true and ignore those that are false. We must do our thing; and our thing is loving, Christlike ministry.

The Lord did not leave us in the dark concerning exactly how we are to go about our work of evangelizing the world and ministering to one another and to persons out of Christ. The Lord himself set the pattern of discipling (empowering, equipping, and training) persons for Christian ministry. He equipped his disciples by showing them how to be loving ministers of Christ's gospel. In the book of Acts, the church continued to grow and spread through loving, Christlike, evangelistic ministry. Later Paul established churches in the cities of the Graeco-Roman world. He gave those churches a strategy and plan for equipping loving, Christlike ministers of the gospel.

> But to each one of us grace was given according to the measure of Christ's gift. . . . And He gave some as apostles, and some as prophets, and some as evangelists, and some as pastors and teachers, for the equipping of the saints for the work of service, to the building up of the body of Christ; until we all attain to the unity of the faith, and of the knowledge of the Son of God, to a mature man, to the measure of the stature which belongs to the fulness of Christ. As a result, we are no longer to be children, tossed here and there by waves, and carried about by every wind of doctrine, by the trickery of men, by craftiness in deceitful scheming; but speaking the truth in love, we are to grow up in all aspects into Him, who is the head, even Christ (Eph. 4:7, 11-15, NASB).

This passage has some great concepts. Every Christian has a gift of Christ and grace enough to exercise that gift in Christ's name (v. 7). All "the saints" (Christians) are to do the work of ministry (serving).

### 3. Priesthood of Believers in Action
The evangelistic church has been greatly harmed by preserving

false traditions that have almost ruled out the ministry of the layperson in the church. We have created a "reverend" class who are in "the ministry." This implies that ministry is off limits for laypersons. The church today needs to take a good look at some of its vocabulary such as "reverend," "ordain," and "clergy" in the light of the New Testament. How much of what we practice in this regard are "traditions of men"? Our churches proclaim loudly the priesthood of the believer. Now we must practice it.

This passage from Ephesians magnifies the role of church leaders. It says that they have been especially gifted by Christ and given to the church to equip the saints to do the work of ministry. The work of ministry is not the religious work done by religious professionals. The work of ministry is Christlike evangelistic ministry that is the task of every believer. Everything that Christ did was evangelistic. He wanted men to have a right relationship to the Father. He healed the sick, fed the hungry, and even raised the dead, but he did it always knowing that he had come from the Father, and that he and the Father were one. The same kind of loving ministry is every Christian's job, every Christian's joy, and will ultimately be every Christian's judgment (Matt. 25:45-46).

## II. The Equippers for Ministry

Gifts for leadership in the early church have significance for today's church. When Paul used the word "apostles," he was not restricting it to the twelve. The word "prophet" was not referring to a special gift that passed out of existence.

### 1. The Gifts of Leadership
In Ephesians 4:8-10, Paul said that the risen Christ, victor over death, hell, and the grave, gave gifts to men and then gave those men to the church as office-bearers or leaders. Some were given the gift to be sent out on special missions. They were "the sent out ones" (apostles). Some were given the gift as prophets with special gifts to apply the word of God to the times in which they lived. Some were given the gift to serve as evangelists. They were gifted in communicating the gospel to those who had not heard. Some have special gifts to know what God is saying to his churches today. They have the gift to make the gospel understandable and meaningful to those outside the church and its influence. To others

he gives the gift to be the pastor-teacher of the congregation. Today the church has missionaries who are sent on special missions. The church has persons especially gifted to apply the word of God to people, social issues, and the life of the nation. We have some persons who feel that their calling and gift is full-time evangelism. All of the office-bearers are given to the church to equip all of God's people for ministry.

### 2. The Pastor-Teacher's Evangelistic Ministry of Equipping

The pastor-teacher is the most important of these gifted office-bearers for the local congregation. In the comforting psalm of Psalms it says, "The Lord is my shepherd." The Vulgate translation says, "The Lord is my pastor." His title indicates his work. He is to shepherd and to teach. The purpose of his shepherding and teaching is to equip. The pastor-teacher has been called by the Holy Spirit and the congregation to lead and equip the whole church for loving, Christlike, evangelistic ministry. This is his responsibility, and there is no way that he can escape it. The pastor-teacher learns from Jesus Christ, the Master Pastor-Teacher. Jesus trained his followers more by demonstration than exhortation. He showed them how. There is today a great deal of emphasis on discipling as a one-to-one process to the exclusion of the group or the congregation. The truth is that Jesus had twelve men in his group. It was more than a one-to-one relationship. They all had relationships with the Lord. The pastor who looks to Jesus as his example will not be discouraged easily. He will know that Jesus sometimes would have to say, "Oh, you have so little faith. I wonder sometimes if you're ever going to understand" (see Matt. 6:30; 8:26; 14:31; 16:8).

It is interesting to see that the disciple relationship of persons to Christ in the Gospels is a teacher-pupil relationship. In Ephesians it is the pastor-teacher who has a major role in equipping the saints to do the work of ministry. The word "disciple" in all its forms is used 231 times in the Gospels, 30 times in Acts, and not a single time in the Epistles. This is far too significant to ignore. The emphasis shifts from the relationship of the believer to Jesus Christ to the relationship of the believer to the church-body. Remember, it is the body of Christ! This is not to say that there is no emphasis on personal relationship to Christ in the Epistles. Jesus "discipled" a group of persons for loving, Christlike, evangelistic ministry. Since the final command of our Lord is "to disciple," we cannot believe

Paul was disobedient to that command or that he chose to ignore it. It really makes no difference whether we say "discipling" or "equipping," or that "we are just getting Christians ready for loving witness ministry." It is referring to the same ministry.

The equipping role is not in conflict with the preaching role of the pastor-teacher. In fact, the preaching ministry of the pastor becomes a vital part of this equipping. The word *equip* is used in the Greek language for outfitting a ship (getting it ready to sail). The word is used for mending (repairing something). It is used for healing (a physician's ministry to a patient). It is used for training (training men for an army). It is not difficult to see the role of preaching in all of these meanings. The greatest thing Christians can say about the preaching of the pastor-teacher is, "Pastor, I learned something today about God," or "myself" or "the world God loves." The pastor-teacher who feeds the flock of God on a steady ration of an exposition of the Word of God will go a long way toward equipping the saints. The people of God need to know how to share the meanings and messages of the Word. The preaching of a pastor who knows how to make the deep things of God plain will be equipping as he preaches. If the saints are fed properly and equipped, they will take care of most of the evangelizing. Pastors are commanded to "do the work of an evangelist" (2 Tim. 4:5, NASB). Equipping is hard work. It will take prayer, study, and commitment on the part of the pastor-teacher.

It is impossible to grow an evangelistic church without a committed, loving, evangelistic pastor. The responsibility for leading and equipping the church in evangelism to obey Christ's command to make, mark, and mature disciples rests squarely upon the shoulders of the pastor-teacher. If the pastor-teacher refuses or fails to rise to the challenge of being a pastor-evangelist in leading, organizing, teaching, and equipping God's people for loving, Christlike evangelistic ministry, he will fail at the very heart of his task. He will fail to lead the church on mission—the mission of Christ, to seek and to save those who are lost. There is no way that the pastor can evade or avoid this responsibility. God wants faithful men, not necessarily men of unusual ability as pastor-teachers. Our faithfulness is predicated upon our ability to commit "the vision" to other faithful men who will commit it to still others. "You, therefore, my son, be strong in the grace that is in Christ Jesus.

And the things which you have heard from me in the presence of many witnesses, these entrust to faithful men, who will be able to teach others also" (2 Tim. 2:1-2, NASB).

### 3. *The Pastor-Teacher's Evangelistic Ministry of Administration*

The pastor-teacher has another title that is full of meaning. He is called a "bishop," or an "overseer" (Phil. 1:1, NASB). This is a word that involves administration. It is used in the Greek language of the New Testament for the overseer of a farm, a bank, or a company. Administration is simply following right procedures to get necessary work done well. In a church with a staff, this task begins with them. In the church with no staff, it begins with the lay leaders of the congregation. The pastor need not do all the equipping. The staff is simply an extension of the pastor's role in the congregation. The minister of education and the minister of music are also equippers for more than just their specialty. They are to equip the people of God for loving, Christlike ministry, not just to sing well or teach well.

I recently saw the business manager of a large church talking earnestly with a young lady in one of the pews of the church and then walk down the aisle with her during the invitation. He was a parable for the whole congregation. He didn't see his task as just balancing the church financial accounts.

The pastor-teacher has to help his whole staff to see that there is an overarching objective—to equip God's people. That objective is more important than good music, good education, or good financial accounting. (This does not mean that these things are not important.) If the pastor has no staff, the lay leaders will have to become equippers along with him in leading and equipping the church for evangelistic ministry. The first chapter of Ephesians is a good example of administration. It presents God's administrative plan for the ages (Eph. 1:10, NASB). There is an objective and then specific actions planned to bring about the objective. In chapter 1 the specific actions are:

1) God's purposive decision *to redeem* before the world began.
2) The provision of a Savior in Jesus Christ.
3) The Holy Spirit's work and sealing act in the believer.

All we have in the church without an administrative plan is cooperative chaos created by organizations competing for their place in the sun. All the church must see that the primary objective is to accomplish its mission. The two decisive acts are evangelizing the unbelievers and equipping the believers. At this point, the Church Administration Department of The Sunday School Board can be a great help to the pastor-teacher.[1]

## III. The Parables of Ministry

We do not owe to Paul all of the debt for the organization and functioning of the early church. The apostles (the twelve) saw a ministry need that they could not meet in the growing congregation. They met that need as the Holy Spirit gave them guidance.

### 1. The First Deacons' Ministry Role in the Church Is Our Example

The function of deacon was created and filled by able men. The seven men that were chosen and believed to be deacons (although they were not called deacons in this passage) continued to be a part of the church organized and functioning (Phil. 1:1). The account is as follows:

> Now at this time while the disciples were increasing in number, a complaint arose on the part of the Hellenistic Jews against the native Hebrews, because their widows were being overlooked in the daily serving of food. And the twelve summoned the congregation of the disciples and said, "It is not desirable for us to neglect the word of God in order to serve tables. But select from among you, brethren, seven men of good reputation, full of the Spirit and of wisdom, whom we may put in charge of this task. But we will devote ourselves to prayer, and to the ministry of the word." And the statement found approval with the whole congregation; and they chose Stephen, a man full of faith and of the Holy Spirit, and Philip, Prochorus, Nicanor, Timon, Parmenas and Nicolas, a proselyte from Antioch. And these they brought before the apostles; and after praying, they laid their hands on them. And the word of God kept on spreading; and the number of the disciples continued to increase greatly in Jerusalem, and a great many of the priests were becoming obedient to the faith (Acts 6:1-7, NASB).

The church was so successful in its evangelism that the ministry needs grew beyond the ability of the twelve to meet those needs. The twelve had a ministry that must not be neglected—the ministry of the Word of God. The church prayed; the men were chosen and approved by the congregation.

### 2. The Deacons Minister to the People of God

They were to meet the ministry needs within the congregation so the apostles could give their time to their ministry. The people in turn would become ministers to those outside the congregation. The first deacons were not an official board formed to conduct church business. They were men who were to be models of ministry for the whole congregation. The thing that is so interesting for evangelism is that the need for the deacons grew out of successful evangelism, and the result of their work was an increasingly effective evangelism (Acts 6:7). The word *deacon* means servant. It is a task more than a title. It is interesting to notice that the first office-bearers of the church were laypersons. They were appointed to meet a practical need.

In the service of the Lord's table, the pastor and deacons engage in a tableau of humility and service. The deacons serve the congregation, indicating that they are the servants of all. If the deacons become a screening committee for the church and lord it over the church or the pastor attempts to make "his will" into "God's will," this tableau becomes a charade. Each must do his work in the church body organized and functioning. The pastor is the leader and the administrator. The deacons are the servants, and the people of God are the ministers. When each plays his God-given role with humility and faithfulness, the church is successful in its evangelism. The layperson is a minister, and the deacons are models for lay ministry. The church that meets the evangelistic challenge of our secular society will have to free every layperson for ministry in the world. It is doubtful that any church can do this if its deacons are out of line with their biblical ministry role. As long as the church sees deacons as "counting noses and dollars," personally responsible for "hiring and firing" pastors, they will not see the great ministry task that God has given to all the church.

### 3. The Deacons Equip Others for Ministry

Deacons that are well organized to meet the needs of the congregation usually have a "flock," consisting of a small number of church families for whom they are spiritually responsible. The Church Administration Department of The Sunday School Board has offered churches in the Southern Baptist Convention effective plans and programs (The Deacon Family Ministry Plan Resource Book [2]) to involve deacons. The Deacon magazine offers continuing help for deacons in fulfilling their role as ministers of the people of God. The deacon becomes a model for the persons in his group. He becomes a model of concern, compassion, and evangelistic zeal. He assists believers with establishing family prayer times, a program of daily Bible reading, and a personal prayer life. When the deacon has one Christian with a family of non-Christians, he accepts direct responsibility for evangelizing the non-Christian members of the family. He guides the new believer in how to become a witness within his own family. The deacon is their minister. He awakens in them the desire to minister. The deacon can then guide his flock into reaching out beyond themselves and their families to minister to persons they meet daily who are out of Christ. Every deacon needs the kind of training offered in lay evangelism schools so that he can assist members of his flock in the techniques of witnessing.

## IV. The Ministers of Ministry

Ministry is a Christian meeting human needs in Christ's name and with Christ's love.

### 1. Ministries Are Inseparable

Paul said to equip the saints to do the work of serving. In the context of the Scriptures, one can hardly separate "ministry" from "evangelistic ministry." All Christian ministry is evangelistic ministry, or it is not Christian. In the life and ministry of Jesus, there was no separation of doing good and doing God's will. There was no division between life and life with God. The early church "went about doing good" in the name of Jesus Christ. A person who gives money to a charity in the hopes that someone may somehow find out that he did it because he is a Christian is living in a dream world. There was no mistaking in whose name and by what authority the church in the New Testament got involved in helping ministries. Laypersons who are Christians must go to the marketplace where men are and minister in Christ's name. The Christian who does good things, never attempting to relate those good things to Jesus Christ, is actually betraying Christ in the marketplace and

There are endless evangelistic opportunities for ministry in the world. Neglected, lonely, confused people all around us need ministry in Jesus' name.

heralding his own goodness.

### 2. *Opportunities for Lay Ministry Abound*

There are endless opportunities for ministry in the world. We can get involved. There are thousands of nonreaders who could be assisted in learning our language in the name of Jesus. There are many social organizations asking for "big brothers" or "big sisters" who can be a pal to some confused, neglected child. Why not become one in Jesus' name? There are many patients in mental institutions who could use a regular visitor and an occasional gift in Jesus' name. Why not get involved? There are great needs for volunteer workers in hospitals, city halls, and in disaster relief. Why not get involved in Jesus' name? There are people all around us hurting. Why not listen in Jesus' name? There are lonely, forgotten senior citizens who need a ride to the supermarket or the doctor. Why not use your car in Jesus' name? The opportunities are as varied as the people who hurt. If evangelistic churches have equipped persons for witnessing, they will find a fertile field in the world.

### 3. *Every Christian Ought to Be a Minister*

The church has been limping along, trying to evangelize a sick, sinful world with a few thousand ordained ministers. What would it be like if every child of God became a minister who took the name of Jesus with purpose and power in loving, Christlike evangelistic ministry? It would be revolutionary. Churches would come alive. Pastors would preach and teach with new vision and dynamics. Missions and evangelism would be more than words that you hear during a stewardship drive. They would become the heartbeat of the church. Every Christian on mission, every Christian an evangelist—is this just a dream? If it is, then Jesus was a dreamer. It is time to pray another prayer from *Creative Brooding* by Robert Raines.

> O God, make me discontent with things the way they are
>    in the world,
>    and in my own life.
> Teach me how to blush again,
>    for the tawdry deals,
>    the arrogant-but-courteous prejudice,
>     the snickers,

> *the leers,*
> *the good food and drink which make me*
>   *too weary to repent,*
> *the flattery given and received,*
> *my willing use of rights and privileges*
>   *other men are unfairly denied.*
> *Make me notice the stains when people get spilled on.*
> *Make me care about the slum child downtown,*
>   *the misfit at work,*
>   *the people crammed into the mental hospital,*
>   *the men, women, and youth behind bars.*
> *Jar my complacency; expose my excuses; get me involved*
>   *in the life of my city,*
>   *and give me integrity once more.*[3]

## Review

What *in the world* is the church for? Is the church only able to offer a pacifier for old people who are afraid to die? What is the church for in the life of persons here and now? The world has said that the church is insensitive to social issues and is always the last to get on the bandwagon of social change and social justice. Jesus Christ came into the world to minister—this is what the church is for. The church is in the arena. Our only weapon is Christ's love. Our authenticating activity is ministry. The Lord has not left us in the dark as to how we are to go about doing "our thing." The great definitive passage is Ephesians 4:7,11-15. Every Christian has a gift of Christ and grace enough to exercise that gift. Every Christian is to be equipped to do the work of ministry.

Some special gifts have been given to the office-bearers of the church. The pastor-teacher of the congregation is the equipper for ministry. This role and gift was given to him by Christ to be used in equipping Christians for ministry. The work of ministry is not the work done by religious professionals. The work of ministry is the task of every believer, and each is to be equipped by the office-bearers of the church. The deacons are models for ministry. The office of deacon was created by a ministry need within and without the congregation. The deacons are not an official board. Their duties are much higher and more spiritual than buying and selling property or hiring and firing the church staff. The people of God are all ministers. There are endless opportunities for ministry in the world. There are public and private agencies crying for help in ministry. Why not get involved in Christ's name?

## Questions for Discussion

1. What *in the world* is the church for?
2. Read Ephesians 4:7,11-15 in the *Today's English Version* (Good News for Modern Man), *The New English Bible,* and/or *New American Standard Bible,* and then discuss what it means. Who are the ministers? Who is to train the ministers?
3. How is the pastor's equipping role an asset to his preaching role?
4. Under what circumstances were the deacons first named in the life of the church?
5. The author defines ministry as "a Christian meeting human needs in Christ's name and with Christ's love." How can Christians minister as individuals?

---

[1] *Leading Your Church in Long-Range Planning; A Church Commitment Planning Guide,* a guide for annual planning; and *Church Development Planbook: a Guide for Annual Planning in a Small Church* may be ordered from your Baptist Book Store.

[2] Order from your Baptist Book Store.

[3] Reprinted with permission of Macmillan Publishing Co., Inc. from *Creative Brooding.* Copyright © Robert A. Raines, 1966.

# CHAPTER 5

I. Foundations for Growing an Evangelistic Church
   1. Vision Precedes Venture
   2. The Pastor-Teacher Shares the Vision
   3. Growing an Evangelistic Church Is a Process, Not a Program
II. Preparation for Growing an Evangelistic Church
   1. Believers Need an Empowering Experience for Evangelistic Ministry
   2. The Empowering Experience Is a Growing Experience
   3. Believers Discover Empowering in a Variety of Ways and Experiences
   4. Equipping Laypersons for Evangelism
   5. Equipping Events and Projects Are a Part of the Process
III. Application for Growing an Evangelistic Church
   1. The Word and the Deed Are One
   2. Evangelism Ministry Meets Humanity's Deepest Needs
   3. Jesus Came to Minister to All People

# 5
# A Strategy for Growing
# an Evangelistic Church

Bill met me at the airport. I was there to preach in revival services in his church. The revival had been in the planning stages for two years. We drove along in silence from the airport, going to the motel where I was to stay. I sensed that something was on Bill's mind. Whatever it was, he was troubled about it. I said, "Preacher, you have something on your mind. Want to share it?"

After a moment of more silence he answered: "I really don't know how to tell you this . . . I haven't used any of the plans you sent me for revival preparation. I'm just sick of 'gimmicks' that we have to use to get people to attend. I'm tired of begging and demanding that my people attend a revival. I'm also sick of bringing in these 'stars' to give their testimony and get a crowd. Christians should come because they want to, because they love people who are not Christians. John, this time I am not going to do anything. We are just announcing the revival, praying, and depending on the Lord, nothing else." Then he added after another lengthy silence: "I sure hope it works. I'm worried about what size crowds we will have."

"This time we will just depend on the Lord." It really sounds good, doesn't it? It sounds so spiritual. It sounds like Bill is no longer depending on "works" and has put it all together in "grace." What Bill had apparently forgotten was that *God was depending on him.* God was depending on his church and every layperson in that church. When the revival week was over, three persons had accepted Christ and requested baptism and two others transferred their church membership. All of them responded during the Sunday morning service of the revival. They were the results of the visitation that Bill and I had done that week. During the week I discovered that evangelism for that church consisted of one or two revivals a year and those that Bill could win through pastoral visitation. The revivals were events when Christians were asked to come and be the spectators and pay for it when it was over. The most involved persons during the week were the two instrumentalists and those who sang in the choir. Even the choir had dwindled to fourteen voices by Friday night. The instrumentalists were relieved two of the five nights so they could take a night off.

This church is exactly like many of our churches. The laypersons in the church are only expected to be the spectators at an "evangelistic meeting." The only assurance that they are involved is the knowledge that their offerings make it possible. This is a weak assurance and a waste of evangelistic potential. During the week Bill and I had a chance to talk about his church. Perhaps the best thing that came out of the meeting was what I was able to share with him about growing an evangelistic church. The greatest asset Bill had was his dissatisfaction with things as they were and a deep desire to have an evangelistic church. I shared three things with Bill that week: a commitment to a study of the Word of God and what it had to say about an evangelistic church; the experience in touching many dynamic evangelistic churches; and a close observation of many of these churches in action. I shared with him some experiences that I had with great evangelistic churches (both large and small, city and rural). I shared with him what I had seen in some churches where people were being converted to Jesus Christ almost daily through the loving, Christlike, evangelistic ministry of laypersons.

One morning after Bill and I had a good prayer experience, I said: "Bill, why don't we talk for awhile. You have shared with me your frustrations about the inability of your church to reach out. You are concerned about the failure of your people to have meaningful relationships with persons out of Christ and out of the church. Let's talk. Let me tell you about some churches I have been in recently." I told him about being the supply preacher in a rather large church on a holiday Sunday. There were eighteen additions to the church that day with the pastor away. Most of these additions were for baptism. Most of them were youth and adults who had no record of church attendance in the past. I said:

"Bill, I found out their secret when I stood at the door shaking hands at the close of the morning service. Person after person came by and asked me to pray for someone they were bringing to the service that night.

"A teenager said, 'Pray for my boyfriend. He is not a Christian. He is coming with me tonight. I have been talking to him about the Lord.'

"A woman said, 'Pray for my neighbor. She is coming with me tonight and is not a Christian. I have been talking to her about Christ.'

"There were at least fifteen people who said the same thing. It is no surprise that seven of the eighteen additions to the church that day responded in the evening service."

I then told Bill about having the same experience in Athens, Georgia, and in New Orleans. I told him about my experience in being a World Missions Day speaker in an evangelistic church. I preached on missions. When the invitation was given, eleven persons responded on a Sunday night. Five of them were professions of faith. All of the professions were adults or youth. The pastor introduced them and asked the person who had been witnessing to them to come and stand beside them. In every case there was a church member who had been instrumental in each decision. I said, "Bill, I am not talking about something I have done. I am talking about something that a growing number of pastors are excited about. I am talking about growing an evangelistic church."

Bill replied, "John, I want that for this church. I want it for myself."

I knew that Bill or anyone else could have what he wanted if he wanted it badly enough to pay the price. I said, "Bill, I know you do. Let's pray now and talk a little more about this later." When we finished our prayer time, I said, "Now let's go make those calls that you have scheduled for today."

For the remainder of the week we visited some Baptists who needed to move their membership, three children whose parents were members of the church, three inactive church members that were husbands of wives who were members of the church. All three of them had formerly been active workers in a church. We also visited some shut-ins who wanted to meet the evangelist.

My next conversation with Bill happened the following day over a cup of coffee in the pastor's study. "John, what is really wrong with our church?" Bill asked. "I preach on missions and evangelism. I pray as hard as I know how to pray. Why isn't this church like some of those you talked about yesterday?"

I answered: "Bill, there is another problem, but let's talk about your immediate problem. I really cannot see that you, your deacons, or the members of your church have any meaningful relationships with the adults and youth in your community who are out of Christ. You have a program and you want people to attend. You ask them to come to worship, organizational meetings, or socials. In your city probably 50 percent of the people have some relationship with a church, sect, or synagogue. They come to things. They come to the religious meetings of all denominations. They have some relationship to a religious group of some kind. They are the "comers." The other 50 percent never come to anything religious except a wedding or a funeral service. This is the group of people you need to reach with your message and ministry. They will not come as a result of an invitation. The people who do come as the result of an invitation have had some kind of religious experience in the past. All of the churches, synagogues, and sects are working on the first 50 percent. Very few of the last 50 percent will ever be reached until they have some meaningful, personal relationships with some Christian."

Bill said: "John, I think I've got it. We've got to switch from 'come' to 'go.' "

"You've got it. But it isn't easy, Bill. You see, so much of our structures are built on the idea of 'come.' Even what we call our evangelistic visitation is nothing more than asking people to come to the church or to Sunday School. That means that we have to have some new concepts, some new structures, and some new relationships."

Bill interrupted abruptly: "Now, John, does this mean that we will do away with Sunday School, WMU, Brotherhood, or Church Training? My people would never stand for that."

"No, it does not mean that, Bill," I answered. "All of the churches that I know who have switched from a 'come' philosophy to a 'go' philosophy have larger organizations than ever before. I am not talking about 'new organizations' but new structures. Those structures feed the organizations. New converts and older ones need to be involved in Bible study, in training for church membership,

llustrate by telling you
mong singles in Atlanta
le. There are thousands
ny of them are divorced
is against divorce and
nta has a large depart-
rch Training. They are
ablish meaningful rela-
lize them. Once these
icult for the 'single' be-
he Blank Baptist Church
he fact that they decided
reached by the church
eased the strength and
was the Sunday School

versation. "Bill, we were
e matter of destroying
evolutionary. I don't buy
way with all the organi-
ers of the house church
ks are trying to 'sell us'
eir meaning and value.'
y of the Home Mission
s still true. He said that
otists is due to our com-
our program of evange-
our teaching on steward-
red missions.

ilures, Southern Baptists
en someone says to me
nizations and start over,

aid. "For a while there
w I would really like to
angelistic church.' "

g on a chapter of a book
It will be published by
of The Sunday School
acon spiritual life confer-

ences in 1977. I'll share it with you."

## I. Foundations for Growing an Evangelistic Church

Jesus Christ had a vision, and he was the vision. In Jesus Christ, the Word and the Deed are one. Jesus Christ who was the Word became flesh (John 1:1,14). Jesus Christ shared his vision with persons who were called his disciples. Later those disciples became the nucleus of his church. Jesus Christ had a vision of an evangelistic church. He spoke an evangelistic church into existence and gave it marching orders from the mount of ascension (Matt. 28:19-20).

If there is to be an evangelistic church, the word and the deed have to be one and the same. We cannot proclaim one thing and live another. The trumpet gives an uncertain sound when our practice contradicts our profession. Yet this is exactly what we do in too much of our church life. We proclaim the priesthood of the believer, but very few laypersons are capable of being an advocate between God and man. In most churches it doesn't even occur to the laypersons that they are to be ministers of Jesus Christ. We proclaim that Christians are to preach the gospel to every creature "as they go." Then our approach to evangelism is too often an invitation to the person out of Christ to come and watch a religious performance. There is today a "new, lean breed" of laypersons in the church who want to get involved in growing an evangelistic church.

### 1. Vision Precedes Venture

The vision must be possessed by and must possess the pastor-teacher of the congregation. If he doesn't have the vision, probably no one else will. To state the vision in nontheological terms is to say that the mission of the church is to evangelize every person who is not a Christian and to equip every person for evangelistic ministry who is a Christian. Lewis A. Drummond in *Leading Your Church in Evangelism* says, "The key to effective mission in this or any other generation rests essentially in the New Testament concept of the ministry of the laity." He says further, "May I be bold and state quite categorically that unless the church recaptures and implements the principle of a lay-centered ministry, I see little hope of fulfilling the commission to evangelize our day." [1] The pastor-teacher must be convinced that the vision God had, that

The mission of the church is to evangelize every
person who is not a Christian and to equip every
person who is a Christian for evangelistic ministry.

Jesus came to make real and gave to the early church, is a vision of the kind of church his church ought to be and can be. An evangelistic church is not a program. It is a vision—a vision that can become a venture.

### 2. The Pastor-Teacher Shares the Vision

If the pastor has a vision of growing an evangelistic church, he will need to share that vision with others. Jesus did this. He shared the vision of who he was and what he came to do with his disciples. It took Jesus many months of demonstrating, teaching, and living to give the vision to a few men. There is no "quickie" way for us to grow an evangelistic church. Churches, however, are different. Some are more responsive than others. If we get discouraged because some do not see the vision readily, remember that Jesus had some problems at this point. Even when he had to leave his disciples alone in the world, they were far from perfection in their perception and understanding of the vision. The pastor has tremendous things going for him in the pulpit. The pulpit is still the most influential forum in the church. Pastor, preach the vision. Give the congregation slices of it in every message. Preach it until their minds and consciences are troubled. Tell them what God envisioned for the world in his Messiah, Jesus Christ. Tell them why Christ came into the world. Tell them that he expects us to complete his mission. Tell them that Christians may serve as airline pilots, truck drivers, business managers, salesmen, waitresses, physicians, lawyers, or whatever to make a living. Being Christian is our profession and calling. Tell them that being a Christian means being like Christ, following in his steps, doing his work, thinking his thoughts. Tell them that the Christian life is an incarnational life—it incarnates Jesus Christ. Footnote every demand to discipleship with the words of Jesus Christ.

Share the vision in small groups with church leaders. The pastor might create a small group of church leaders that he feels may be most susceptible to the vision, including some deacons, youth, Sunday School teachers, and others. Call it an evangelism study group or evangelism sharing group. Use this book or Leading Your Church in Evangelism by Lewis A. Drummond as a base, or just use the New Testament. Trace what Jesus did and said. Study the activities of the church in the book of Acts. Apply the teachings to the life of the group and the church. If the church has a staff, begin sharing these things with them in staff meetings. Make prayer a definite part of these small group meetings. Let the hunger grow as the Spirit of God begins to work. It is interesting to notice that Jesus waited until one man saw the vision before he spoke the church into existence (Matt. 16:18). When Peter saw that Christ was the Messiah and all that this implied, Jesus was ready to give him more revelation and responsibility. When there are enough persons who begin to see the vision of growing an evangelistic church, it will be time to talk about how to do it.

### 3. Growing an Evangelistic Church Is a Process

One of the great temptations is to go on with the "how to" before we settle the "why" in our minds and hearts. This is the reason so many evangelism programs "fizzle out" in the church. A church can have a lay evangelism school, and it really is a "fun" project. As soon as it is over, the church may be the same. The same is true of a revival, Renewal Evangelism Weekend, or YES (Youth Evangelism Strategy). A vision alone cannot sustain evangelism as a continuing process. The church has to see that growing an evangelistic church is not a program. It is a process. It is a vision. It is a lifetime commitment. There can be no turning back. Two things are apparent when we begin to see the layperson in the church as an evangelistic minister. The first is that the average layperson has a great deal more desire to be directly involved in this kind of a life-style than we give him credit for. Second, the average layperson requires a great deal more help to become a consistent, evangelistic minister than we suppose he needs. This is the reason it is important that we see the vision and make a lifetime commitment to it.

## II. Preparation for Growing an Evangelistic Church

As we have studied in this chapter, there are three phases in growing an evangelistic church: foundations, preparation, and application. They should not be viewed as successive stages where we complete one stage and go to another until we complete them. These phases must be seen as constantly recurring cycles. All three are constantly going on in the evangelistic church. The vision neglected is soon forgotten. Preparation discontinued means stagnation and routine duty rather than inspired service. Application neglected results in words without deeds and vision without venture.

When we talk about preparation for growing an evangelistic church, we are not talking about replacing traditional and effective tools for evangelism that Southern Baptists have used. We do not mean that we will no longer see the Sunday School as a great evangelistic tool of the church. Indeed, what we are talking about would make the Sunday School officers and teachers a dynamic force for evangelism in the life of the church. We do not mean that churches will no longer need revivals. What we are talking about would make revivals take on new meaning and purpose. We would not be just talking to ourselves. We would see all organizations and projects as a part of the evangelistic process. The organizations and the projects of the church would be seen as a part of the process of helping persons to see the vision, preparing persons for evangelistic ministry, and assisting persons to apply the vision in loving, Christlike evangelistic ministry.

### 1. Believers Need an Empowering Experience

Believers need to be prepared for evangelistic ministry in an experience of empowering. The early Christians in the New Testament were not to begin their task of world evangelization immediately, but they were to stay in the city until they were "clothed with power from on high" (Luke 24:49, NASB). Their empowering experience was an experience with the Holy Spirit that gave the vision venture (Acts 2:1-4). God doesn't want us to go in our own strength. Growing an evangelistic church is more than pastoral drive, initiative, and ambition. It is more than effective administration, good educational programs, or just meeting the needs of persons. It is the calm, quiet, but dynamic faith that we are not alone in our venture. We know that Christ's last promise to his church was that if we would "go" he would be with us in the person of the Holy Spirit. Paul prayed that the Ephesians would know this kind of empowering experience.

*I pray that the eyes of your heart may be enlightened, so that you may know what is the hope of His calling, what are the riches of the glory of His inheritance in the saints, and what is the surpassing greatness of His power toward us who believe. These are in accordance with the working of the strength of His might*

*which He brought about in Christ, when He raised Him from*
*the dead, and seated Him at His right hand in the heavenly places,*
*far above all rule and authority and power and dominion, and*
*every name that is named, not only in this age, but also in the*
*one to come. And He put all things in subjection under His feet,*
*and gave Him as head over all things to the church, which is*
*His body, the fulness of Him who fills all in all (Eph. 1:18-23,*
*NASB).*

### 2. An Empowering Experience Is a Growing Experience

Paul piles word upon word and phrase upon phrase as he describes the kind of power that believers are to experience. We are to know (actually experience) "the surpassing greatness of His power." This is according to "the strength of His might." Human sinfulness had done all it could to eliminate Christ, but God "raised Him from the dead." His power is greater than human sin or diabolic power. This is the kind of power the church needs when it deals with human sin and rebellion. It is this power that is to clothe believers in their work of evangelistic ministry. As Paul thought of his own ministry, he said that he was gifted for his ministry "according to the working of His power" (Eph. 3:7, NASB). After Paul had spoken to the Ephesians about their life and work in the church body, in the home, and in the world, he said, "Finally, be strong in the Lord, and in the strength [power] of His might" (Eph. 6:10, NASB). The greatest enemy of Christian witness and ministry is fear. Paul says to Timothy, "For God has not given us a spirit of timidity, but of power and love and discipline" (2 Tim. 1:7, NASB).

### 3. Variety in Empowering Experiences

The empowering experience comes to believers in different ways and in different times. It is not a once for all experience. There is a real sense in which we need daily empowering. Some persons have found this experience of renewal in a revival service. Others have experienced it in a genuine act of rededication in a worship service. Many youth are experiencing empowering in Joy Explosions and young adults in Agape Feasts. Others testify to this kind of an experience in a Lay Renewal Weekend or in becoming related to a small renewal group.

In one church recently a meeting of the deacons turned into

a renewal session that changed the direction of the lives of several deacons. There is no question about the importance of the small group concept as an aid to self-discovery and renewal. We need to look at a continuing process of empowering that includes events and projects. A good example is a spiritual retreat for selected groups such as the adult Sunday School teachers. As we look at the process, we must be certain that no groups of persons in the church are neglected. Besides spiritual retreats we can consider Lay Renewal Weekends, Renewal Evangelism Weekends, Joy Explosions for youth, and other activities as being on our agenda. Revivals having purposes other than evangelism, such as Deeper Life Revivals emphasizing personal relationships in the church, the home, the place of work, and the world, might be included in the schedule. Small groups integrated into existing organizations could carry a continuing thrust as persons are assisted on their spiritual journey.

### 4. Equipping Laypersons for Evangelism

Equipping believers is just as important as empowering in preparation for growing an evangelistic church. As we have previously said, Jesus discipled persons for loving, Christlike evangelistic ministry; and Paul equipped persons for loving, Christlike evangelistic ministry. The discipling process of Jesus included both empowering and equipping. Again we cannot say, "O.K., this person is now empowered and is ready to be equipped." It is not as sequential as that. Indeed, the two are continuing things in the life of the growing Christian and a part of the process of growing an evangelistic church. In a previous chapter we have discussed the classical equipping passage from the fourth chapter of Ephesians. We cannot expect laypersons to be minsters of Christ without giving them help any more than we can expect them to be a part of the professional ministry without help. There is no need to open theological schools to train laypersons. The church itself must do the equipping. We need to have training opportunities in counseling, witnessing, teaching, biblical studies, and ministering. The church curriculum may need renewal at this point. The equipping studies should not get bogged down in all the technicalities of theological jargon. Laypersons do not need to study Greek and Hebrew. They don't need to master all the theories of theology. Indeed, they will be more valuable if they retain their "lay language" which is more likely to communicate with the secular world. Colleges and seminaries should continue providing a curriculum to equip the pastor to be an equipper of laypersons.

### 5. *Equipping Events and Projects*

The Lay Evangelism School and YES (Youth Evangelism Strategy) have been very successful in some churches as a tool in the process of equipping laypersons. The Lay Evangelism School and YES major on equipping in the area of witnessing. Churches that have used these two activities as regular projects in their equipping process have reported good results. One church has had eighteen schools in three years. Some churches trying these schools as a "one shot" project have been disappointed in the continuing involvement, even though the week of the school may have been effective. One church has trained five deacons and five deacons' wives in witnessing and counseling. They work with persons, problems, and needs at the front of the worship area, leaving the pastor free to give the invitation. Persons trained in this way will find many opportunities to minister to persons with problems outside of the life of the church. A church with a television program found that it had more calls for hospital visitation than the pastor could take care of. That church equipped six deacons in witnessing and the art of hospital visitation. Today they are making far more hospital calls than the pastor. They visit persons who are not related to the church. The pastor and staff still make most of the hospital calls to members of the congregation. Equipping must be going on all the time. It must be for specific tasks and functions. Christ has given us gifts. The church can help persons use their gifts.

## III. Application for Growing an Evangelistic Church

First the word and then the deed. This is the Jesus way. The word without the deed is sham and hypocrisy. Jesus came into the world to minister and to die (Matt. 20:28). Unless self dies, one cannot be a minister of Jesus Christ. Ministry is applying the vision, the empowering, the equipping to people where they hurt.

### 1. *The Word and the Deed Are One*

Words are so easy and so cheap, and the church has been long on words. John R. Mott, in speaking to a great missions conference, said that it is a dangerous thing to glow with a knowledge of the needs of men, to be swept by generous emotions, if that knowledge and emotion do not issue in genuine action. He urged that the end of the conference be the beginning of conquest. As far as we know, Jesus never once said to any person, "I love you." Yet his every deed was one of love. He was love. The church has yet to discover its greatest evangelistic tool—ministry. Here is a prayer we can pray together:

> Grant us the will to fashion as we feel,
> Grant us the strength to labour as we know,
> Grant us the purpose, ribbed and edged with steel,
>   To strike the blow.
>
> Knowledge we ask not—knowledge Thou hast lent;
> But Lord, the will—there lies our deepest need.
> Give us to build above the deep intent,
>   The deed, the deed.[2]

### 2. Ministry Meets Humanity's Deepest Needs

Ministry is meeting humanity at the point of humanity's need. It is touching a person where he hurts. I have made a point that all Christian ministry is evangelistic, and if it is not evangelistic, it is not Christian. Witnessing is ministry to man's spiritual need. Always there is in the mind of the believer that necessity to bring God into the problem. A person's most basic need is for God. The critical issue of humanity is a right relationship with God. If evangelism is adding members to "my church," then all ministry is not evangelistic. But evangelism is not adding members to "my church." Evangelism is presenting Christ in the power of the Holy Spirit so that men will come to accept him as Savior and serve him as Lord in the fellowship of his church.

Paul Benjamin says in his book, How in the World, "The New Testament clearly teaches the ministry of all believers. Only as that doctrine moves from a theory in the congregation and becomes a part of practice can there be any hope of a worldwide spiritual revolution."[3]

### 3. Jesus Came to Minister to All People

Ministry does not ask persons to "come and do our thing with

All around us are gap groups that the church has missed. They represent millions of persons who are responsive to loving ministry.

us." Ministry goes to those who would never come. When believers have the vision and are empowered and equipped, they can apply the word in the deed. All around us are gap groups that the church has missed. They represent millions of persons. They are responsive to loving ministry. There are many churches in the Southern Baptist Convention that have already discovered the joy of meeting human needs in the name of Christ. Jesus said, "I did not come to call the righteous [to repentance] but sinners" (Matt. 9:13, NASB). They are out there—the alcoholics, the drug addicts, the cheaters, the swindlers, the liars, the thieves. Jesus came to minister to them. The Home Mission Board has resources that churches can use to assist us in our ministry to these persons. Jesus said, "People who are well do not need a doctor, but those who are sick" (see Matt. 9:12). They are out there in the world where we live, move, work, and play. They are out there—the night people, the divorcees, the parents of handicapped children, the internationals, the senior citizens, the troubled children. We must go where they are. We must apply the "balm of Gilead" to hurting humanity. If we are to do this, we must die, that Christ may live in us. All that is human rebels against the death of self. How can we forget "not to be ministered unto, but to minister" (Matt. 20:28). Ask God to deliver us from always thinking about persons in terms of what they can do for us. Pray with me another prayer of Robert Raines from *Creative Brooding:*

> *I am like James and John,*
> *Lord, I size up other people*
>    *in terms of what they can do for me;*
>    *how they can further my program,*
>      *feed my ego,*
>      *satisfy my needs,*
>      *give me strategic advantage.*
> *I exploit people,*
>    *ostensibly for your sake,*
>    *but really for my own sake.*
> *Lord, I turn to you*
>    *to get the inside track*
>    *and obtain special favors,*
>      *your direction for my schemes,*
>      *your power for my projects,*

> your sanction for my ambitions,
> your blank check for whatever I want.
I am like James and John.

> Change me, Lord.
> Make me a man who asks of you and of others,
> what can I do for you? [4]

## Review

Bill and John discussed the evangelistic church. Bill found out that he needed to turn his church from a "come" structure to a "go" structure. The church needs to have foundations for growing an evangelistic church. It is important that the pastor have a vision of an evangelistic church and that he is able to communicate the vision to others. The pastor shares the vision with deacons and/or other leadership groups. The church must settle the "why" before they get to the "how to." The three stages of growing an evangelistic church are foundations, preparation, and application. The three must not be seen as sequential but as a continuing process that we are involved in even simultaneously.

This new way of structuring "go" actions is not a threat to the established organizations of the church. It should mean that the organizations are being constantly strengthened. Equipping believers does not mean that we will no longer need revivals. Equipping believers will give revivals new meaning and vitality. Part of the preparation for growing an evangelistic church is empowering. We are not to go out in our own strength. The earliest Christians were told to wait for the enduement of the Spirit. There are many events in which individual believers can find empowering experiences such as revivals, retreats, lay renewal weekends, renewal evangelism weekends, Joy Explosions, Agape Feasts. Equipping events such as the lay evangelism school can play an important role in the equipping process. Application is the point at which the word becomes the deed. Unless what we do is applied in loving, Christlike evangelistic ministry, the process has no meaning.

## Questions for Discussion

1. What kind of feelings do you have about Bill and his church? Do you think Bill is typical of many pastors?

2. Is the "vision" as important in your thinking as the author seems to think?
3. How can the pastor effectively share his "vision" of growing an evangelistic church with his church leaders?
4. Read Ephesians 1:18-23 and discuss the kind of empowering believers need for Christian ministry.
5. What events and activities can the church schedule in the process of empowering and equipping believers for ministry?

---

[1] (Nashville: Broadman Press, 1975), pp. 59-60.
[2] Reprinted by permission of Curtis Brown, Ltd. Copyright © 1919 by John Drinkwater. All rights reserved.
[3] (Lincoln: Ill.: Lincoln Christian College Press, 1973), p. 63.
[4] Reprinted with permission of Macmillan Publishing Co., Inc. from *Creative Brooding*. Copyright © Robert A. Raines, 1966.

# CHAPTER 6

I. The New Testament Principles for the Evangelistic Church Organized and Functioning
  1. The Church Is God's Only Instrument for World Evangelization
  2. The Church as the Body of Christ Has Only One Head
  3. Jesus Christ Has Given the Church Gifts and the Grace to Use the Gifts
  4. The Church Is the Body of Christ Ministering to Its Members
  5. The Church Is the Body of Christ Ministering to Persons Outside the Church
  6. The Church as a Body and as Individual Members Will Reproduce Themselves in New Believers and New Churches
  7. The Pastor-Teacher Is to Reproduce Himself
II. The Evangelistic Church Understanding Its Own Needs
  1. A Spiritual Survey of the Congregation
  2. Interpreting the Survey
III. The Evangelistic Church Setting Measurable Goals
  1. Convening a Goal-Setting and Planning Group
  2. Setting Measurable Goals and Determining Actions
IV. Evaluating Results for Efficiency
V. Answering Three Vital Questions
  1. Why Begin with the Church?
  2. What Is the Relationship to Church Organizations?
  3. Why Emphasize Christian Social Ministries?

# 6
# The Evangelistic Church Organized and Functioning

*And Simon Peter answered and said, "Thou art the Christ, the Son of the living God." And Jesus answered and said to him, "Blessed are you, Simon Barjona, because flesh and blood did not reveal this to you, but My Father who is in heaven. And I also say to you that you are Peter, and upon this rock I will build My church; and the gates of Hades shall not overpower it. I will give you the keys of the kingdom of heaven; and whatever you shall bind on earth shall have been bound in heaven, and whatever you shall loose on earth shall have been loosed in heaven" (Matt. 16:16-19, NASB).*

*And He put all things in subjection under His feet, and gave Him as head over all things to the church, which is His body, the fulness of Him who fills all in all (Eph. 1:22-23, NASB).*

*I therefore, the prisoner of the Lord, entreat you to walk in a manner worthy of the calling with which you have been called, with all humility and gentleness, with patience, showing forbearance to one another in love, being diligent to preserve the unity of the Spirit in the bond of peace (Eph. 4:1-3, NASB).*

*But to each one of us grace was given according to the measure of Christ's gift (Eph. 4:7, NASB).*

*For no one ever hated his own flesh, but nourishes and cherishes*

*it, just as Christ also does the church, because we are members*
*of His body (Eph. 5:29-30, NASB).*

*For through the grace given to me I say to every man among you*
*not to think more highly of himself than he ought to think; but*
*to think so as to have sound judgment, as God has allotted to*
*each a measure of faith. For just as we have many members in*
*one body and all the members do not have the same function, so*
*we, who are many, are one body in Christ, and individually members*
*one of another. And since we have gifts that differ according to*
*the grace given to us, let each exercise them accordingly: if prophecy,*
*according to the proportion of his faith; if service, in his serving;*
*or he who teaches, in his teaching; or he who exhorts, in his*
*exhortation; he who gives, with liberality; he who leads, with*
*diligence; he who shows mercy, with cheerfulness (Rom. 12:3-8,*
*NASB).*

The key to growing an evangelistic church rests with how the
church is organized and functions. This key is a little more difficult
to put our hands on simply because it is not a "given" key from
the New Testament. The theological and visionary keys are to be
had by believers who give themselves to serious study of the New
Testament and the life, mission, and ministry of our Lord. Churches
are not so much in a theological crisis as they are in a crisis of
effectiveness. There are thousands of churches who are sound in
their beliefs but really quite ineffective when it comes to making
an impact upon a secular society. Beyond the very basic, simple,
primitive New Testament organization of the church, the New
Testament does not provide a detailed plan for us to make an
impact in a modern world. Jesus warned that it was hard to put
"new wine into old wineskins [bottles]." The communities that
churches exist in today are complex with very few social forces
holding them together and many forces driving them apart. We
cannot expect to take the methods used by the churches in the
New Testament or the churches of the nineteenth century to evangelize the world today. The principles remain the same but methods
change.

How effective is our church? This is a pressing and pointed
question for all pastors, deacons, and other church leaders. How
many of our additions to the church last year were by letter? How

many did we baptize? How many of those baptized were above fifteen years of age? How many of those baptized were children of our own members? How many non-Christians above fifteen are presently involved in some ministry of the church? Though these questions focus on our ineffectiveness in evangelizing, they do not tell the whole story or the most important story.

A whole new set of questions needs to be focused on the church itself. How many Christians witness regularly in their daily lives? Does the church reflect the unity of the body of Christ (Eph. 4:1-2)? How many church members practice a consistent prayer life? How many persons in our congregation read their Bibles devotionally each day? Do they care about one another? There are other questions, but these serve to point up some of the needs. When we ask these questions in the light of population gains and the increasing number of people who are unreached by our ministries, we realize a need for more effective efforts.

The reaction of church leaders may be to say, "How about Evangelism Explosion? We have heard that it really works." A committee goes off to Florida to study it. Or the church leaders may say, "What we need is a lay evangelism school. They had a great one at the Seymour Street church. Perhaps the pastor there would come over and help us have one." Other church leaders may say, "The Church of the Savior in Washington is reaching people through coffee houses. Let's start one in our community." Others may say, "We need a Lay Renewal Weekend. What we need is to get the church turned on. I heard that they had one at Jones Avenue church, and it was successful. They had people laughing, crying, and hugging one another until they couldn't dismiss the morning service. It lasted until 2 o'clock." Still others may say, "We need discipling. We need to find out who the 'apostles' are in the church and let each one of them disciple another. I heard they really are doing things with discipling at that church on Moore's Mill Road."

Sound familiar? It would be humorous if it were not so tragic. All of the things mentioned are programs. They are tools and they are good tools. But all that these programs will lead to for many churches is disillusionment with programs. When a program was suggested as a solution to the evangelistic needs of a large church, a layperson, who was a member of the evangelism committee, said, "If you are telling me about another program, stop! I have programs up to my neck." He did not have the answer, but he knew that another program was not the answer. The answer is the New Testament church organized for and functioning in evangelism.

## I. Principles for the Evangelistic Church Organized and Functioning

The principle of the wheel is as sound today as it was in New Testament times, but we do not use oxcarts for transportation. The wheel is continually being refined and updated. Today we must constantly update our efforts to meet contemporary needs based on New Testament principles for an organized and functioning church.

### 1. *The Church Is God's Only Instrument for World Evangelism*

The first principle is that the church is God's only instrument for accomplishing world evangelization. There are mission societies, evangelistic associations, Christian media people, and interdenominational evangelistic movements. Many of them work along with and beside the churches and are generally known as "parachurch movements." They could not exist without churches. Most of their resources come from people evangelized by the churches. Indeed, if churches were doing what they ought to do, there would probably be no reason for parachurch movements. Sending twenty-five people to take training in a parachurch organization may be also just another "program." Only the church's existence is guaranteed by an age-long commission. Our Lord committed himself and the task of world evangelization only to his church. As a prerequisite to evangelism, the church needs the reassuring conviction that the world's only chance to hear the saving truth of the gospel depends on their faithfulness. The church cannot expect anyone else to accept its commission given by our Lord. We cannot ignore the masses of humanity on our church fields. If we fail them, there is no other plan. God doesn't have another team waiting on the sidelines if it appears that we will lose the game.

### 2. *Christ Only Is the Head of the Church*

The church as the body of Christ has only one Head. Jesus Christ is Lord. He is the Head of the body, the church (Eph. 1:22-23).

The church is a live, functioning, organized body. The church is to receive directions from him. He is to us "wisdom from God" (1 Cor. 1:30, NASB). Christ knows how the churches can become effective in their communities. His wisdom is available to us in prayer and through the ministry of the Holy Spirit (John 16:13). An aged evangelist of another generation said to me, "John, every great evangelistic church that I have seen in the world had one thing in common—they mastered the secret of prayer." We must be in touch with Christ. The body provides oxygen and nourishment to the head, giving it life. The head gives direction and organization to the body, assisting it to function. The church body of Jesus Christ makes him live in the world. Jesus Christ gives wisdom and direction to the church body so it can function effectively. This union with Jesus Christ, though mystical, is very practical. The church body must see through the eyes of Jesus Christ. Living in mystical union with Jesus Christ, the church body sees sinning people as the creation of God worth dying for and worth witnessing to.

### 3. Jesus Gives Gifts and Grace to Use Them

Jesus Christ has "gifted" his church to perform its functions in the world. We have already looked at the passage in the fourth chapter of Ephesians where Paul told how Christ "gifted" men as office-bearers of the church with the abilities to equip the saints to do the work of ministry (Eph. 4:12). In 1 Corinthians 12:28-30; Romans 12:3-8; and 1 Corinthians 12:8-10, we discover some areas of spiritual gifts given to believers so that the church can function. These gifts are for the people of God. Paul said that it is very important that we have a knowledge of spiritual gifts (see 1 Cor. 12:1).

1) The gift of preaching (prophecy) is for proclaiming God's revelation of himself in Jesus Christ.

2) The gift of wisdom is to know the will of God in all matters that concern the church and others.

3) The gift of faith is to channel the blessings of God into the lives of others.

4) The gift of teaching is to make plain the Word of God and its claims upon us.

5) The gift of the utterance of knowledge is to make eternal truth plain and to apply it to everyday life.

6) The gifts of the Holy Spirit—mercy and loving-kindness—are to allow the love of God and the compassion of Christ to flow into other lives.

7) The gift of discernment of spirits is to make clear whether or not our motives are pure.

8) The gift of administration (governments) is to keep order in the life and work of the church and the believer.

9) The gift of useful helps is for ministries to others in need in the church and the community.

10) The gift of healing is for special ministries to the ill and suffering.

11) Special gifts are for special signs of God's presence and power.

Since church members have been given gifts and the grace to use those gifts (Eph. 4:7), it follows that church leaders must assist them to use their gifts. This is a principle from the evangelistic church of the New Testament that applies to evangelistic churches today. We must take the promise of Christ at face value and assist every member of the church body to discover and use his gift. Some churches operate on the principle that pastors and a few laypersons have all the gifts and about all the other members can do is to attend, pray, and give. The figure of the body and all its members in 1 Corinthians 12 teaches that every member of the church body has a "gifted" role in the body organized and functioning.

4. *The Church Is the Body of Christ Ministering to Its Members*

The word that best translates the New Testament word "fellowship" is sharing. It is a principle of New Testament churches organized and functioning—that they share themselves and all that they have with one another. This ministry of sharing is extremely important for evangelism. It is especially true for "body language." The church in the New Testament impressed the pagan world because they loved one another. The nonverbal communication of the church to the world is, Here are people who really care about one another. You won't need church signs or newspaper ads that read, "Come to the church that really cares." The community will know it. The persons in the congregation who have discovered their gifts and the grace to use them can then minister to fellow Christians with wisdom, useful helps, knowledge, and teaching.

5. *The Church Is the Body of Christ Ministering to Persons Outside the Church.*

Our ministry to one another is the proving ground for a larger ministry to non-Christians. This ministry is not for the purpose of getting new church members or even making converts. It arises from Christlike compassion for people who are hurting. The end result will be persons converted to Jesus Christ in most cases. We are not to decide who will or who won't become a Christian. Jesus ministered to needy persons without questioning whether or not they would follow him. Evangelism will be the overflow of lives blessed by his living in them. The result will be a new life-style that dies to self in Christlike ministry (Matt. 20:28). This is imperative for the evangelistic effectiveness of churches.

The Home Mission Board Evangelism Section had scheduled an area revival crusade in a small city in a new state convention where Southern Baptists were almost unknown. A small attendance of less than a hundred persons was expected. The crusade began with five hundred persons and the crowds increased. What happened? Between the scheduling of the crusade and the date it was to begin, the small city had a disastrous flood. Another department of the Home Mission Board, without knowing about the planned crusade, gave money for rehabilitation and sent volunteers to work in rebuilding homes and cleaning up. The word became the deed and bore evangelistic fruit.

6. *Church Members and Churches Are to Reproduce Themselves*

The New Testament principles of reproduction for the church organized and functioning is vital in evangelism. The church is a body and its individual members are to reproduce themselves. Churches reproduce churches and believers reproduce believers. There is no way to separate what has come to be known as "church growth" from evangelism. Churches will reproduce churches. Evangelistic churches will reproduce evangelistic churches. Churches can become so large that they make evangelism reproduction difficult. For example, some large churches that report over a hundred baptisms during a five-year span actually have a smaller ratio of baptisms per members than some rural churches that report no baptisms for some of the five years. There can be no reproduction of churches, however, that is significant unless there is first the basic reproduction of believers within the body. No church can really be alive to its full potential in a New Testament sense that is satisfied only with additions by church letter and baptizing their children.

### 7. The Pastor-Teacher Is to Reproduce Himself

There is another area of reproduction that both church-growth people and evangelism people have neglected—the pastor-teacher reproducing himself. Every evangelistic church has a significantly larger number of young people feeling and accepting God's call to missions, evangelism, and the pastorate. The three practical, pertinent questions are: Are there an increasing number of believers in our churches who are reproducing themselves? Do our churches have a desire and a plan to reproduce themselves in another church body? Are young men and women in significant numbers feeling and responding to God's call to professional vocations in missions, evangelism, and local church vocations? Evangelistic churches are growing churches; and growing churches evangelize unbelievers, nurture believers, start new churches, and encourage and motivate youth to accept Christ's challenge to professional careers in growing evangelistic churches around the world. Now suppose we review our principles:

1) The church is God's only institution for accomplishing world evangelization.
2) The church as the body of Christ has only one Head, Jesus Christ.
3) Jesus Christ has "gifted" his church to perform its functions in the world.
4) The church is the body of Christ ministering to one another.
5) The church is the body of Christ ministering to persons out of Christ and out of the church.
6) The church as a body will reproduce itself in new churches. Christians will reproduce themselves in new believers.

## II. Understanding the Needs of the Congregation

Rebirth, like judgment, must begin at the house of God. There is no need to think about the outreach of the church to unbelievers until we begin to meet some of the needs of believers. If evangelism is every Christian's job, then there must be some reason why Christians are not performing the task. One oil company made a lot of mileage out of the motto, "It's performance that counts." God will hold every church and every believer responsible for their performance (Luke 12:41-49). If every Christian has been given gifts and the grace to use those gifts, why isn't he using them?

### 1. A Spiritual Survey of the Congregation

One of the best ways to find out is to take a survey. The survey can be a very useful tool in getting needed information. It is not an end, but a means to an end. We want to find out exactly why people are not performing. The results of the survey may be shocking to the pastor and church leaders. In our denomination surveys have been taken, speeches delivered on their findings, and often nothing is ever done with the information. We are particularly adept at producing a frightful array of statistics on increasing unbelief in the world and urged on to "work for God." In many instances nothing comes out of it all because·nothing changed the condition of the church. Our first principle is that the churches (local and visible) are God's instruments for world evangelization.

There are several crucial areas in which we need data if we are to discover the needs of the congregation. What is the level of biblical truth necessary for the vision and the theology? Does the individual member have an adequate level of biblical knowledge that will provide the spiritual resources to understand and perform in evangelism? We need to determine the level on which persons operate in relationship to prayer, the Holy Spirit, forgiveness of sin, and the church. We also want to probe in the area of the Christian life. For several years we have been emphasizing "lifestyle" in the Southern Baptist Convention. We want to know about attitudes, opinions, prejudices, and mind sets. We want to determine the attitudes of members toward the church and fellow Christians. They may not feel a need to minister to persons who are not Christians because they have never been ministered to. We want to know something about people in the areas of outreach, including witnessing, leading others to faith in Christ, acts of social concern, witness, and personal ministry. We will also want to know whether or not they are resistant to change. The following suggested survey of the church membership can be easily reproduced and taken at a morning worship service or at some other appropriate time.

Using the "Congregational Survey Form, 'This Is Really Me'" can provide some needed data to discover the degree to which church members are practicing evangelism.

## Congregational Survey Form—"This Is Really Me"

**Note:** This survey is about you. You do not need to sign it. Check whether you agree or disagree that this statement is you. The larger the box you check, the more strongly you agree or disagree with the statement.

|  | Agree | Disagree |
|---|---|---|
| 1. I believe every Christian should be a witness. | ☐ ☐ ☐ | ☐ ☐ ☐ |
| 2. I think we should try some new ways to worship. | ☐ ☐ ☐ | ☐ ☐ ☐ |
| 3. My family prays together as a regular part of our home life. | ☐ ☐ ☐ | ☐ ☐ ☐ |
| 4. I worry a lot about money. | ☐ ☐ ☐ | ☐ ☐ ☐ |
| 5. I rarely miss a good show on TV. | ☐ ☐ ☐ | ☐ ☐ ☐ |
| 6. I have some very close friends who are not Christians. | ☐ ☐ ☐ | ☐ ☐ ☐ |
| 7. I feel uncomfortable when I talk to people of another race or culture. | ☐ ☐ ☐ | ☐ ☐ ☐ |
| 8. I don't understand a lot of things the preacher talks about. | ☐ ☐ ☐ | ☐ ☐ ☐ |
| 9. When I do wrong, I confess my sins to God. | ☐ ☐ ☐ | ☐ ☐ ☐ |
| 10. People who have problems often come to me to talk. | ☐ ☐ ☐ | ☐ ☐ ☐ |
| 11. I feel that I am getting the spiritual food I need from our worship services. | ☐ ☐ ☐ | ☐ ☐ ☐ |

|  | Agree | Disagree |
|---|---|---|

12. I talk to people about Jesus Christ quite often.

13. I think a person's religion is his business, and I shouldn't "bug" him about it.

14. I help needy people quite often.

15. My home and children take up so much of my time that I really can't do much else.

16. The greatest joy I have is leading some person to decide for Jesus Christ.

17. I have found people in the church to be my greatest help when I have problems.

18. I would enjoy some training in how to share my witness for Christ.

19. I think the worship services are very dull and boring.

20. I think we pay preachers and staff members to do religious work like witnessing, and they ought to quit asking me to do it.

21. I think there have been many times when I felt that the Holy Spirit had complete control of my life.

22. There are a lot of things wrong in my life, but I never do anything about them.

|  | Agree | Disagree |
|---|---|---|
| 23. I read the Bible every day, and it makes me stronger spiritually. | ☐ ☐ ☐ | ☐ ☐ ☐ |
| 24. I get a lot of spiritual food from the preaching in our church. | ☐ ☐ ☐ | ☐ ☐ ☐ |
| 25. I think Christian social ministry is important for the church. | ☐ ☐ ☐ | ☐ ☐ ☐ |
| 26. I think most poor people are lazy and need to go to work. | ☐ ☐ ☐ | ☐ ☐ ☐ |
| 27. I sincerely like people. | ☐ ☐ ☐ | ☐ ☐ ☐ |
| 28. If people would just clean up their own doorstep and leave others alone, we would be all right. | ☐ ☐ ☐ | ☐ ☐ ☐ |
| 29. I think owning a good home and automobile and having a good job are very important for my happiness. | ☐ ☐ ☐ | ☐ ☐ ☐ |

## 2. Interpreting the Survey

This kind of a survey will help church leaders to discover what kind of persons the church is developing. One can easily check records and discover how well members attend meetings and contribute, but records tell us very little about the kind of persons they become. It is important that the survey be a personal evaluation. The questions that are asked can vary. It is important that the questions be both positive and negative so the answers can be cross-checked. Some significant questions can be answered out of the survey. Are the members of our church adopting a Christian life-style? Are they equipped for ministry to others in and out of the church? Do they witness with any degree of regularity? How many are capable in their own thinking of leading another person to a decision about Jesus Christ? Are the church services exciting and motivating? Is their knowledge of the Bible sufficient to assist them in seeing their responsibility?

Once the survey forms are completed and interpreted, you are ready to take another step. Before we do, let's review our steps in an evangelistic church organized and functioning:

1) Understand the New Testament principles.
2) Understand the needs of the congregation.

## III. Setting Measurable Goals for the Congregation

The survey has spoken to us about the audience. The goals and plans must speak to what we have learned about the audience.

### 1. Convening a Goal-Setting and Planning Group

We are now ready to convene an evangelism goal-setting and planning group. It can include the deacons, the church council, youth leaders, and Sunday School outreach leaders. At this point we are in peril from "programitis." When the needs are presented, there will be immediate pressure for a revival, a lay evangelism school, a Lay Renewal Weekend, LIFE, AGAPE, or some other program as the patent answer for all that ails the church. Our churches are program-oriented. It will not be easy to break the pattern. If we have done our homework, we can come to this group with the survey results interpreted. We can pull out of the survey several areas of felt need. We should not pick programs that may or may not have worked in other places. We should try to meet felt needs in our congregation. To circumvent the group's getting into an endless discussion of programs, interpret to the planning group the results of the survey. Point out the three or four areas of felt need that are now present in the congregation. Point out the fact that real one-to-one evangelism is impossible for many members of the congregation until their needs have been met.

Recently a survey of evangelism leaders was taken in states and associations. They were asked to give reasons why churches were not reaching persons out of Christ. The following are the first five of ten reasons given:

1) The failure of Christians to witness for Christ as a matter

of daily life-style
2) The neglect of Bible reading and prayer in the lives of many Christians
3) The breakdown of the family altar and the Christian home
4) The lack of a caring relationship between members of the church body
5) No sense of responsibility for people who are hurting outside the fellowship of the church

Before going on, take just a moment and relate the five reasons above to the six New Testament principles for an evangelistic church organized and functioning. It is almost certain that a survey of felt needs in any congregation that is not growing will surface these five reasons with variations. Daily witnessing, devotional life, the Christian home, caring relationships in the body, and Christian social concern are the points at which our people are crying for help.

### 2. Setting Measurable Goals and Determining Actions

Divide the planning group into five work groups, each one having an assignment for one of the concerns. Impress upon them that Christ is the head of the church, and he has some directions for us. Each work group should be clearly instructed to develop some measurable goals and some suggested actions to meet the goals. Do not hurry the process. It may take several meetings of the larger group and the planning work groups until a consensus that reveals the mind of Christ has been concluded.

One of the significant areas of need relates to witnessing. Some pastors say only 3 or 4 percent of their congregations include consistent witnessing as a part of their Christian life-style. Look at the Congregational Survey Form again. The answers to questions 1, 12, 16, 18, and 20 will reveal the needs of the congregation related to witnessing. Suppose that only 16 percent indicated that they witness with any kind of consistency. Suppose that 80 percent felt that witnessing is the business of the "religious professionals." It might be a measurable goal for a response of 25 percent to strongly affirm, "The greatest joy I have is leading some persons to decide for Jesus Christ by one year from today." One action might be to involve 58 persons in an evangelism training event such as a lay evangelism school in the next three months. Another measurable goal may be to have one hundred persons accept Christ

and unite with the church through the personal witness of members
during the coming church year. There would need to be many
actions in order to meet such a challenging goal. Some of the actions
would need to be in areas of empowering and equipping. The
final work of the committee might look like this:

I. *Witnessing*
  A. *Goals*
    1. During the next twelve months, to have 25 percent
     strongly affirm the statement, "The greatest joy I
     have is leading some person to decide for Jesus
     Christ."
    2. During the next twelve months, to lead one hundred
     persons to Jesus Christ and church membership through
     the personal witnessing of our members.
  B. *Actions*
    1. To preach a series of sermons (at least four) on the
     obligation of Christians to witness.
    2. During the next three months, to plan, schedule, and
     conduct at least one witness-training event, such as a
     lay evangelism school.
    3. During the next three months, to plan, schedule, and
     conduct special prayer and teaching sessions for Sunday
     School outreach leaders.

II. *The Devotional Life*
  A. *Goals*
    1. To have 50 percent of the congregation strongly affirm
     the statement, "I read the Bible every day and it makes
     me feel stronger spiritually," within the next twelve
     months.
    2. To begin twenty small groups for Bible study and prayer
     within the next six months.
  B. *Actions*
    1. Ask Sunday School teachers to emphasize daily Bible
     reading in the Sunday School record system.
    2. Use the WIN booklet, "The Devotional Life," as studies
     for the twenty small groups.
    3. Make available to any who will use it the small book
     *Time Alone with God* by Barry St. Clair (Arthur Davenport

and Assoc.).

III. *Christian Family Life*
   A. *Goals*
      1. To have 40 percent of the congregation strongly affirm the statement, "My family prays together as a regular part of our family life."
      2. During the next twelve months, to lead 32 parents (of children attending our church) that are either not Christians or not church members to make the proper decision for Christ.
   B. *Actions*
      1. To initiate and/or strengthen the Deacon Family Ministry Plan during the next three months.
      2. Send *Home Life* magazine into every home that has one or more members of the family who are members of our church.
      3. To conduct a Christian Home Revival in the church within the next six months.

IV. *The Caring Church*
   A. *Goals*
      1. To have 40 percent of the congregation strongly affirm the statement, "I have found people in the church my greatest help when I have problems," within the next twelve months.
      2. To initiate some sharing-caring small groups who discover the secret of affirming one another in personal needs within the next three months.
   B. *Actions*
      1. To plan, schedule, and conduct a Lay Renewal Weekend and renewal evangelism activities with continuing sharing groups within the next six months.
      2. To preach a series of sermons on "The Sharing Church" within the next three months, using some of the material in chapter 2 of *The Evangelistic Church.*

V. *Christian Social Concern*
   A. *Goals*
      1. To have 30 percent of the congregation strongly affirm

the statement, "I think Christian social ministry is really important for the church," within the next twelve months.

2. To have 100 members of the congregation actively involved in some kind of Christian social ministry within the next twelve months.

B. *Actions*

1. Organize some special Christian ministries groups to the following "gap groups" (people who are ordinarily overlooked by the church)—alcoholics, poor, teenagers in trouble—within the next six months.

2. Survey the community to discover groups of persons who are overlooked.

The above actions only represent suggested goals a church can take in a typical situation. Prayers and creative thought will enable the large planning group and the work groups to recommend goals, projects, and activities for growing an evangelistic church. They will not be preoccupied with programs. The survey can reveal many needs. It can reveal a weakness in the pulpit ministry. (See statements 8, 11, and 24.) The survey can indicate a need to change the forms and content of worship. (See statements 2, 11, and 19.) Some may feel that the survey is not directly evangelistic. Remember that a person in the congregation may not be involved in witnessing because of a lack of prayer, personal problems, or a lack of needed spiritual food. The lack of witnessing is only the symptom. We want to get at the disease. Now let's review again our steps in the evangelistic church organized and functioning:

1) Understand the New Testament principles.

2) Understand the needs of the congregation.

3) Set measurable goals.

## IV. Evaluating Results for Efficiency

At regular intervals progress should be measured to determine the degree of effectiveness. The same congregational survey should be made again at the end of a year. If it is obvious that suitable progress is not being made, plans can be evaluated by the large planning group and the work groups even before a year has gone by. We are involved in a process, not a program; we are interested in the effectiveness of the process. Any or all of the programs are expendable. When we evaluate activities, projects, and programs, the acid test must be their lasting effectiveness. Too often we judge the success of evangelistic projects on the basis of crowds, statistical success, or the spiritual "highs" it produces. Without depreciating any of these, we still must ask, How much have these projects contributed to our short- and long-range goal to grow an evangelistic church?

Flexibility is important. Our ability to change is important because we operate in a changing society. The methods that worked in the past are not necessarily the methods that will work today. What works for one church in one community may not work for another church in another community. We must discover for ourselves what will work for us. Love will find a way. When the church is the church, it is evangelistic. It is just as natural as breathing. Some of the new and exciting ways to reach people have been discovered by churches that just did what their hearts told them to do. Reaching persons out of Christ is easy and natural when churches decide to be Christ's body doing "his thing" in the world. The early churches did not work at being creative. They just kept in touch with the Holy Spirit, who is God's agent in creation and creativity.

Now for our final review of the steps in an evangelistic church organized and functioning:

1) Understand the New Testament principles.
2) Understand the needs of the congregation.
3) Set measurable goals.
4) Evaluate results.

## V. Answering Three Vital Questions

There may be some questions in the mind of the thoughtful student of evangelism.

### 1. *Why Begin with the Church?*
Almost the totality of this book is directed to the local church and the individual believer. This emphasis must be repeated. Our failure in evangelism is not a failure of *doing*. It is a failure of *being*. The classical pun is to refer to churches as "God's frozen people." This phrase has even been used as a title for a book on the failures of churches. The Christian and the church are on

mission. The mission is Christ's mission. Being a Christian is incarnating Jesus Christ. We need to recover the word "revival" in its Old Testament sense as a rebirth of the people of God. Evangelism is not the cause but the result of a spiritual church. In a church where the springs of spirituality have gone dry, evangelism is an impossibility. There is little joy and celebration in many of our services of worship and a great deal of dull and routine exercises. But the spirituality of the church is not made by us. It is the creation of the Holy Spirit. The Spirit uses the communication of the truth from the pulpit, prayer, and the Word in bringing about a spiritual church. This book, then, deals with churches because when a church is right it will evangelize.

### 2. What Is the Relationship to Church Organizations?

Another question may well be asked, "What is the relationship between what has been said in this chapter and the organizations of the church such as Sunday School and Church Training? Many of us received a great deal of empowering and equipping in both Sunday School and Church Training during our early ministries. Some people who are "hooked" on discipleship today have forgotten that teachers and leaders in church organizations have been discipling for a long time. The Sunday School is a very important evangelistic strategy for churches today. Church Training affords a great deal of training for evangelism. New Member Orientation is an important part of church evangelism. The Brotherhood organization leads out in Lay Renewal Weekends that have made significant contributions to the personal renewal of many Christians. WMU and Church Music make great contributions to evangelism in faithfully teaching our mission responsibility. The more evangelistic a church becomes, the healthier these organizations will be.

These organizations, however, are not evangelism in themselves. A church could have all the organizations and not be evangelistic. Some Christians feel that their "busyness" in church organizational life makes them evangelistic. The organizations need renewal as well as persons. Their renewal comes when persons in them no longer see them as ends within themselves, but as tools the church has available to do better work in witness and ministry in the world. The real task of the church is not keeping the organizations manned. It is witness and ministry in the world. It is so easy for us to substitute organization for the living organism of the church.

The life and work of the church is the important thing. Sharing our life in Christ with one another and with the world is the important thing. Organizations are the structure we use to teach the Word of God and to train believers for effective ministry and witness. Organizations must be measured by the yardstick of effectiveness. The church is on mission in the world. How we accomplish this mission will change with the times. For this reason organizations, like institutions, are in need of renewal. There are encouraging signs that the church organizations are now in process of renewal. To this end we must pray and work.

### 3. Why Emphasize Christian Social Ministries?

A third question may be in the mind of the thoughtful student of evangelism. Why so much emphasis on Christian social ministries? One of the healthy signs about our organized life in the Southern Baptist Convention is that evangelism and Christian social ministry are housed in the same agency at the Home Mission Board. There has been a healthy interaction that has almost buried the polarization of believers into two camps of "soul-savers" and "do-gooders." The emphasis that has been placed upon ministry in this book is both biblical and Christlike. The place of Christian ministry is in the world. We witness by our caring love. This witness is not only to the unbeliever; it is also within the structures of society itself. To witness within the structures of government means that some Christians are present in government who understand government. They are there to witness and use whatever means possible to bring needed change based on what Jesus said and did. He is there to report to the churches what he sees and feels. Watergate might have been averted if Christians in the highest levels of government had stubbornly insisted on being the incarnation of Jesus Christ. No Christian can be like Jesus Christ without being both evangelist and minister. As Paul said to the Corinthians in regard to the second Palestinian relief offering, "Now therefore perform the doing of it" (2 Cor. 8:11).

### Review

This chapter is about an evangelistic church organized and functioning. The organization and function of the church grows out of six New Testament principles. They are:

1) The church is God's instrument for evangelism.

2) Christ is the Head of the church.
3) Christ has given the church gifts and the grace to use the gifts.
4) The church is to minister to one another in the body.
5) The church is to minister to persons out of Christ and out of the church.
6) Christians will reproduce themselves in new Christians, and churches will reproduce themselves in new churches.

The church organizations and functions are to meet the needs of the members of the church body. One way to discover needs is to take a survey. At this point the church must not make the mistake of seeing some programs as a quick solution to meeting the needs of the church.

When the church has discovered its needs, it is ready to adopt some measurable goals and to take some actions to meet those goals. All of the goals speak to the needs of people. All of the actions reflect ways we intend to reach the goals. The results of the survey are interpreted to a large planning and goal-setting group composed of deacons, members of the church council, youth leaders, and others as needed. The large group is divided into five work groups to consider goals and actions to meet five felt needs of the congregation. Prayer is to be a major part of all meetings of the large group and the work groups. The group seeks to have "the mind of Christ," who is the Head of the church. Goal setting and action planning are considered for five areas of felt need; witnessing, the devotional life, Christian family life, the caring church, and Christian social ministry.

The next step in the evangelistic church organized and functioning is the evaluation of the results of the survey. The final criteria is effectiveness in reaching goals. Programs represented in projects and activities are considered expendable for the sake of effectiveness.

In the final paragraphs, three questions are answered. The first question is, "Why begin with the church?" The failure of churches in evangelism is not "doing" but "being." Churches that fail to meet Christ's expectations do not have the spiritual resources for mission. Our efforts to grow an evangelistic church must begin with the church itself. The second question involves the relationship of this chapter's content to the church organizations. The Sunday School, Church Training, and the other organizations have been used of God in empowering and equipping church members for witness and ministry. Organizations must not be seen as ends within themselves. The task of the church is not keeping the organizations manned, but accomplishing the mission of Christ in the world. The final question deals with the relationship of evangelism to social ministry. We witness as believers by our caring love. We care about people, society, and the world. Christians cannot be like Jesus Christ without being both evangelist and minister.

## Questions for Discussion

1. Look at the passages of Scripture at the beginning of this chapter. Can you locate the author's six New Testament principles for an evangelistic church organized and functioning?
2. In what ways do we discover ministries to persons out of the church by ministering to fellow believers in the church?
3. Look at the survey form on page 107. Does it give us a spiritual picture of ourselves?
4. Discuss measurable goals for evangelism in your church. If you desire you can do some role playing as a "Church Planning and Goal-Setting Group."
5. Do you agree with the author's statement, "If we are like Jesus Christ, we are both evangelist and minister"? In what ways are we evangelists and ministers?
6. Do you feel strongly that Christian social ministry and evangelism are important parts of our Christian witness?

# Notes